D0936404

IF ONLY I COULD SLEEP
MY NERVES ARE ALL ON EDGE
I SHALL BE IN A TERRIBLE STATE TO-MORROW
WHAT WOULDN'T I GIVE FOR A GOOD NIGHT'S REST!

Say
Good-bye *to* Sleepless Nights

THOSE dreadful nights when you toss and turn—think and worry—far into the small hours. How they wreck your nerves, undermine your health and ruin your good looks!

And it is all so needless, since there is a sure, pleasant way to get sound, peaceful sleep every night. Just drink a cup of delicious 'Ovaltine' at bed-time. It is remarkable the way 'Ovaltine' soothes your nerves, composes your mind and quickly leads you through drowsiness to deep, health-giving sleep.

Furthermore, 'Ovaltine' builds you up while you sleep. It is supremely rich in lecithin to strengthen the nerves—carbohydrates to re-create energy—vitamins and other vital nutritive elements to restore the whole physical system to glowing health and fitness.

Try the 'Ovaltine' way to-night. See how soundly and peacefully you sleep—how refreshed and vigorous you awake—how fit you feel for the work of the day. But it *must* be 'Ovaltine'—there is definitely nothing "just as good." Reject substitutes.

Drink delicious
'OVALTINE'
The World's Best Nightcap

Prices in Gt. Britain and   N. Ireland, 1/1, 1/10 and 3/3

P342A

Bed Manners

A VERY BRITISH GUIDE TO

Boudoir Etiquette

DR. RALPH HOPTON & ANNE BALLIOL

Published in Great Britain in 2014 by Old House books & maps
c/o Osprey Publishing, PO Box 883, Oxford OX2 9PH, UK.
c/o Osprey Publishing, PO Box 3985, New York, NY 10185-3985, USA.

Website: www.oldhousebooks.co.uk

A CIP catalogue record for this book is available from the British Library.

ISBN-13: 978 1 90840 291 2

The material for this book was first published in 'Bed Manners' (1936) and 'Better
Bed Manners' (1936), by Ralph Hopton and Anne Balliol, with illustrations by
Evelyn Cockayne.

Printed in China through World Print Ltd.

IMAGE ACKNOWLEDGEMENTS
The Advertising Archives, cover image; Alamy, pages 1 (right), 2, 96 and 152; Getty
Images, page 24; Mary Evans Picture Library, pages 1 (left), 10, 82, 126 and 139.

14 15 16 17 18   10 9 8 7 6 5 4 3 2 1

The material reproduced in this book was first published in the 1930s, and
contains the common spelling and terms used in everyday language of that period.

Contents

HOW TO USE THIS BOOK

WHAT? A new etiquette book in a world already groaning under the weight of thousands of etiquette books? Yes. Because this book pioneers in a new field of good manners and good form. It goes straight into the bedroom. It discusses bediquette, the new social science intended for people so clever that they do not just hang up their good manners every night with their clothes. This is the first complete book on how to be knightly, nightly. We commend this subject to every intelligent reader as an important new branch of public beducation.

Of course, you may be living all alone on a desert island, to which you have fled to escape your creditors, your wife, or the like. If so, it doesn't matter how you behave at night. Only the owls and fireflies can see you, and it makes no difference to them if you snore, mutter in your sleep, kick the clothes off the bed, or commit any other breach of social etiquette. But probably you are not alone, or don't want to be.

Civilized life is full of strange adventures. Some people explore the jungle, others work in laboratories with deadly germs, others get a kick out of polo, or mountain climbing, or cruising in deep water in tiny boats like cockleshells. But the strangest adventure of all is to find yourself locked in a bedroom with a person of the opposite sex, with whom you are required to go to bed and get up thousands and thousands of times. This is called "marriage." It may have happened to you already. Or it may happen just when you least expect it and are least prepared.

Very well. How are you going to act? How are you going to make the other person act? The schools teach many valuable subjects like geometry, ancient history, football and algebra, but they do not teach bed manners. As a result, young people plunge into marriage with no idea how to behave.

During the past year, to prove our point, we have studied more than one million words written by every authority on etiquette. We have listened to the radio as well. Make this test yourself, and what do you get? You get a lot of information about visiting cards, and lawn fêtes, and the right way to eat asparagus, and how to write a letter to a public man, and to set the table for a formal luncheon. This is all good, as far as it goes. But it never goes past bedtime. You might think these authorities wanted you to sit up all night writing formal letters, or practising the correct way to grip asparagus, or something.

Now, you know better than that. You know that you can't sit up all night for more than a few nights without feeling very tired and wanting to get some sleep. Very well. This little book which you are now reading tells you, in a few practical lessons, everything you need to know about good form in the bedroom. Knowledge is power.

Grasp it firmly, and you will be able to remodel the behaviour of the person who sleeps with you. This person has no doubt been behaving very badly, for lack of good, practical information, such as this book supplies. If this is not checked, at once, it will lead to quarrels, injured feelings, and eventually to divorce. You probably will not be able to afford a divorce this year. Avoid all such expense by leaving this book in some place where your bedfellow will see it and absorb its lessons. If it doesn't work a cure, nothing can.

If you wish to do good in your community, like a good citizen, you should extend the usefulness of this book by giving it to every married couple who are beginning to crack under the strain. In the very next home in your street, you may have reason to know that the husband is a boor. Or the wife may behave as if she had been brought up in the monkey-house at the zoo. Your course of action is obvious. Buy a copy of this book and leave it on their pillow. They may be surprised when they see it, but they will thank you in the end, when they learn how much happier it will make them.

You have a duty to young people, too. Instead of letting them grow up and marry in blind ignorance of the natural pitfalls caused by imperfect bed manners, you must see that a copy of this book goes to every prospective bride and bridegroom. A young woman who finds it among her wedding presents will appreciate your kind thought. So will the college student who receives it as a prize from you.

Another splendid use of this book is as a gift to your physician. He meets dozens of discontented married people in his daily rounds. He will want to prescribe this book to all of them, as soon as he has read it, digested it, and learned what it can do to make his own married life bearable, even happy.

One word of warning. This is the first and only book ever printed about *Bed Manners*. The subject is a vast one. The happiness of many million people depends on it. Therefore, do not attempt to read this book rapidly. Meditate each chapter before you take up the next one. You must think as you read. You can do this in the privacy of your home, or in the subway, or out riding with friends, or in odd moments at the office or factory where you work. Carry it about with you and *give its magic a full chance to work*.

1

A Short History of Bed Manners

PREHISTORIC BED MANNERS

Perhaps the best way to treat this subject is to quote a report made by that famous scientist, the late Dr Alonzo Blodgett. He spent seven years making a study of the manners and customs of the South Sea Islanders for the Ethnology Department of Siwash University. His final report was brief. It merely read "They have no manners and their customs are disgusting."

PRE-BED BED MANNERS

During a large portion of Man's historical life bed manners did not exist. This was due to the absence of beds. Life was simple in this period. At the end of the day people lay down and slept. If not eaten by tigers, they walked off at dawn. The only courtesy one could show to one's cave chum was not to step on him (or her).

BED MANNERS IN THE DARK AGES

The first beds were really rooms within rooms. They had roofs from which hung heavy draperies like sleeping-car curtains. These air-tight folds surrounded the entire structure. The question of who was going to open the window did not exist in the good old days. This fabric sarcophagus occupied the centre of the great upper hall in every well-appointed castle. On the floor and benches surrounding it slept the court: ladies-and-gentlemen-in-waiting, pages, hautboys, halberdiers, friends of the family, serfs and serfants – anyone, in fact, who couldn't find a better place. All snored together in an amiable hodge-podge. This phenomenon was never repeated until the advent of the sleeping car.

Upon retiring, My Lord and Lady merely waved good-night to half a hundred people and dived through the curtains. If they were King and Queen, however, they were not allowed even this privacy. A loyal band of ladies-and-gentlemen-in-waiting immediately dove in after them. Then followed the royal unbuttoning and unlacing, undoubtedly accompanied by much shouting and innocent laughter. The royal clothes were whisked away. The happy couple were at last alone – prisoners until their clothes were brought back with the dawn. But the court slept around them on floor and couches, all night long.

Under these conditions bed manners were necessarily restricted. Conversation was addressed, not to the royal bedfellow, but to the straining ears on the other side of the curtains. The system had its advantages. If a courtier became too clubby it was only necessary to remark "Yes, dear, Sir D'Arcy's a nice boy, all right. He's a bit fresh though. To-morrow morning I'm having him put on the rack. That'll straighten him out." In the morning you could count on Sir D'Arcy being well on his way.

On the other hand the opportunities for private conversation were about equal to those in a modern broadcasting studio. If the arrangement was trying to King and Queen, however, what must it have been for the ladies-and-gentlemen-in-waiting on the sofas and divans? As time went on they began to drift away to the nunneries and monasteries. There at least they had private cells. Desertions became so alarming that bedrooms were finally installed in every home by royal decree.

EARLY FRENCH BED MANNERS
(FOR ADULTS ONLY)

We touch on the levée in another part of this work. The custom originated in France and rapidly spread to other places. French customs frequently do. To give a levée, an eighteenth century lady of fashion merely yelled "Come in!" and then tried to get a negligée on before the room filled up with male friends for conversation and hot chocolate.

Obviously bed manners were limited in this period. If any of the gentlemen had possessed good sense and breeding, they would have been down at their offices supporting their families, instead of hanging around other women's bedrooms.

With the French Revolution the art of elegant conversation vanished. Young blades, at loss for what to say, took to tweaking the bedclothes off. Levées were abandoned. They have only recently come back.

EARLY BED MANNERS

Bed manners have passed through many crises. One of the most acute was brought about by the custom of *Bundling*. To understand this practice we must realize that no people have ever had a stricter code of morals than our ancestors. Even more deeply planted in these grim souls, however, was thrift. If a daughter didn't marry she must be supported. No suitors, no marriage. Even the most ardent suitor refused to freeze to death in pursuit of love. Fuel was scarce and dear. Necessity, the mother of ideas, gave birth to Bundling. Necessity now has a lot of granddaughters, but these are outside the scope of this study.

Under the Bundling code both parties went to bed with their clothes on. NRA (No Removals Allowed) was strictly enforced. The very act of getting into bed with one's clothes on, however, is so contrary to all good manners that further comment is unnecessary.

THE DOUBLE BED IN ECONOMIC LIFE

The double bed was first used because most people were lucky to have any bed at all. It was not until the depression of '96, however, that the brilliant French inventor, Lits Jumeaux, gave to mankind the twin bed. The sleeping habits of the civilized world

15

changed overnight. The demand for twin beds became insatiable. The country emerged from industrial stagnation and misery into an era of prosperity which lasted until the Great War.

Sheet and blanket mills went from zero to double shifts. Acres of virgin forests fell heavily. Mattress hair became so scarce that the cotton stuffed mattress was widely used, bringing prosperity to the land. The remainder of the unemployed were kept busy carting old double beds to the dumps.

MODERN BED MANNERS
There are none. But if this little book doesn't give your spouse a rough idea of how to act at night, we advise you to keep a pet instead.

2

The Great Problems of Marriage

ADVICE TO THOSE ABOUT TO MARRY

WE BEGIN this chapter with a frank statement that it leaves a lot of ground uncovered. It isn't so much for bachelors and spinsters, of all ages, as it is for people who have plunged right into matrimony in the good old English spirit of learning an art just by practising it. Never once in all the former books about etiquette has there been a word about pleasing the one person whose displeasure most affects your life. Say "Good night" properly to the Joneses. It doesn't matter, apparently, whether you say "Good night" to your wife, or hit her over the head with the fire bucket. Up to now, people have laboured under the delusion that it is unimportant what happens behind bedroom doors, so long as there is no scandal. This is a mistake. Anyone who has ever attended breakfast at a house party, following a red-hot bedroom argument between the host and hostess, knows this to his own discomfort.

Outside the bedroom we received an intensive training in the art of living with our fellow human beings without lynching or being lynched. Nurses, parents, teachers, professors all concentrated on this single aim. Never were we free from "Don'ts" and "Do's," with this one exception. Once in our own room instruction ceased.

Small wonder then that we find ourselves unprepared to cope with the situation after marriage. Neither party has ever been properly bedroom broken. When you add to this complication the fact that most modern couples see little of one another outside of the bedroom for periods of twenty, thirty and forty years, the seriousness of the situation becomes apparent. If both parties to what is optimistically known as the marriage contract should behave towards one another before marriage with half the rudeness they display after it, there not only would be no wedding bells, but even the front-door bell would have rung only once. Do you think Cleopatra ever let Mark Antony see her trying to wriggle into her under-garments? Imagine any heroine in the books by popular novelists giving the judge an earful about her Man leaving his smelly-welly old pipe on top of her freshly laundered lingerie!

Bad bed manners are cumulative in their effect. The husband who hops into his conjugal nest a bit potted, on one night, will be forgiven. Let him do it two nights running, or six nights, or thirty nights, and see how much mercy he can win.

Neither has been properly bedroom broken.

If you will preserve the twin principles of being both mannerly and charming in bed, you can go forth on your matrimonial career without fear. You hold the key in your hands. Every day begins with a couple of people getting out of bed. Every day ends with those people crawling into it again. That is where charm begins and ends. Even if you don't carry it about all day with you, like a handbag or brief-case, you need it – and lots of it – all night.

Charm is the glue that holds marriages together. Charm is your passport to the best houses and the best bedrooms in those houses. You may be as ugly as a toad, you may not know how to eat asparagus, your toes may be sticking out of the ends of your boots – but if you have charm, your wife will rank you with Galahad, Apollo, Andrew Carnegie and Rudolph Valentino.

IN BED WITH A NICE PERSON

Perhaps this experience is still ahead of you. Without this book to put you on guard, you would have some very rude shocks. You surely have memories of sleeping in youth with a large, soft teddy bear. Or was it a doll? Or a kitten? You naturally expect your human sleeping partner will be as soft as the teddy bear, as quiet as the doll, as gentle as the kitten.

The surprise that will come to you may be the most terrible in your life. Not one of your expectations will come true.

So perhaps it is just as well if you happen to be a friendly, old-fashioned, matey kind of person from a large family where flocks of guests were always being invited to spend the night. You were always being doubled up with a sister or brother. Or one of the little guests was shoved right into bed with you. Then you know what to expect. Human anatomy is no surprise to you.

It is to the absolute beginner in sleeping double that this chapter is addressed. Your first shock will come from the discovery that even the nicest person – even a plump, handsome, really beautiful person, once voted by his friends the handsomest man at Oxford – is actually a skeleton most insufficiently padded at the forehead, chin, shoulders, elbows, hips and knees.

And if your prospective bedfellow is a lady – yes, even a lady who has put on five pounds since she won a beauty contest at Folkestone in 1933 – why, even this buxom bedmate is also a skeleton with no padding whatever at the points we have mentioned above. Such grievous wounds can be inflicted by the bony forehead, the sharp chin, and the hard shoulders, elbows, hips and knees that their use is strictly illegal in the prize-ring.

Crash! comes your bedfellow's elbow into the tender place just below your ribs. Or smack! comes his knee into the small of your back. He doesn't mean anything by it. He is just "turning over in his sleep."

This is the moment to toss him out of bed and then have a short, intimate chat with him on the subject of lying quiet. But suppose he is a nice person, and was bed broken long ago as the result of living in a large family with too few beds for all the people who used his home as a free lodging house.

He is just "turning over in his sleep."

He is quite likely to tell you that the female skeleton is just like the masculine one – only a bit sharper at the corners, and at the ends of the fingers. He may say gently that he wishes you would keep your claw out of his eye. You didn't mean to put it there. You just thrust out your arm as a defence mechanism against a mosquito. (You can almost hear the mosquito give a low, hoarse chuckle of satisfaction as your husband rubs his eye.) We seem to be bearing down hard on this skeleton matter. That's because it is so unexpected to all beginners in bedmanship. Although they have taken their own skeletons to bed with them every night of their lives, it is a merciful provision of nature that you can't stick your elbow in your own eye, or deal yourself the so-called "kidney punch" with your own knee.

The very nicest people, by the way, often have a "skeleton in the cupboard." That's the nicest place for it. Hang it up there and it may rest peacefully for years. But if you must have it on you at all times, then learn to control it.

Bedfellows soon get tired of being butted, gouged, slugged and otherwise maimed. They put their heads together (without enough of a bump to produce two fractured skulls) and work out a rough set of Queensberry Rules for their own protection.

But what are some of the other great surprises in your beducation?

THE ENCROACHER

Perhaps you have married an "encroacher." He is the sort who unconsciously shoves you, inch by inch and foot by foot, across the bed. He doesn't know he is giving an imitation of a star player in a Rugby scrum.

He is sound asleep. You become aware of him, dimly, when you feel his jaw against your neck, or his clenched fist in the region of your spine. You groan, and move away. Instantly he occupies the captured territory. In military language, he consolidates his position. Perhaps he gains another four inches by breathing heavily on the back of your neck. You move. He leaps into the place you have just occupied. Very soon you are on the absolute edge of the bed. You are teetering on it, ready to plunge. Now you have what is called "the falling dream." You think you are plunging down, down into space. And you will plunge, if your funny old encroacher has his way with you.

Long-suffering people at this point try to foil the encroacher by climbing over him. This feels a good deal like changing places in a Canadian canoe. But you manage it. You have a faint hope that the encroacher will keep on travelling in his original direction, with the happy result that he will crash to the floor himself. You hope he will. Vain hope! He will come right back after you, now prodding, now pushing, until he has driven you across the centre-line of the field (pardon us, the bed). Now you are on your five-yard line, now on your goal-line, and there is nobody present to shout "Hold 'em!"

What to do. A lot of wives want to solve this problem by using a revolver or a heavy sashweight. Even if they had to stand trial as the result, they say it would be far less of a trial than what they have gone through.

THE HUMAN CATERPILLAR

Another sort of bedfellow is really a caterpillar in disguise. In his sleep he grabs all the bed-clothes and winds them round himself like a cocoon, leaving you bare.

You wake, chilled to the bone. You find this great human caterpillar snoring away beside you. You unwind him. With chattering teeth you remake the bed. You fall into stupor, only to find that he has done it all over again.

What a pity that, if you left him to himself, he would not emerge from his cocoon as a beautiful butterfly. But he won't. No wings will ever sprout on him. In the morning, when you are sneezing and shivering in the first stages, of pneumonia, he will wake up smilingly and say: "Where did you get that snuffle, Gwendolen? I slept as warm as toast all night."

READERS-, TALKERS-, AND
EATERS-IN-BED

These are minor afflictions. You can bilk a reader out of his or her secret joy in your sufferings by installing a spotlight. Of course, he or she can't be allowed to read a newspaper that rattles in your ears like musketry. A book is better. Also duller – so it will put the reader to sleep much faster.

Choose bedside books for their soporific qualities. Follow the advice of the stupidest assistant in the worst bookshop in town. Avoid all the good detective stories. Tell the library man you want volumes of serious importance. Poetry is a real lullaby to most people, and a "stream of consciousness" novel is nearly as good a sleep-producer as the trickle of a real stream outside your window.

As for the talker-in-bed, never argue with her. That only wakes her up, brushes the cobwebs out of her eyes. She may say the most bitter things about your earning capacity, about your relatives, about the bad habits the children have inherited from you. Agree with them all. Agree with grunts and other sounds indicating that you are very, very sleepy. Turn the conversation into a monologue. Most monologues you ever heard put you to sleep, didn't they? In the morning, refrain from asking whether the little monologuist beside you is talking still or again. Just spring nimbly up, with no questions at all.

Now for the eater-in-bed. A lot of women regard breakfast in bed as the one supreme luxury of their lives. During the honeymoon period (the twenty-four to seventy-two hours which follow one's wedding) she may invite you to share this meal. Suggest two trays and two tables, one on each side of the bed. A deluge of hot coffee is painful, and bad for the sheets. So is a fumbled egg, while a muffed muffin will deposit crumbs where they can irritate you most.

As for the miscreant who keeps stuff on the bedside table to nibble or munch at night, hanging is too good for him. Fill the stomach with food in the evening, and you will get through to breakfast all right. Try to peel an orange, on your back, and it will squirt accurately into your bedfellow's eye. Try to eat a biscuit without showering crumbs into the bed. The sharp deposit of grit from this source will make any night sleepless.

These are the common types of bad bedfellows. Avoid them or reform them. There is no middle ground.

SEVEN GREAT PROBLEMS
OF MARRIAGE

Hurrah! You are in bed. The day is over. The Wiffenpoofs' dinner is over too, and you have many hours of blissful slumber ahead of you. Your night clothes are becoming. Your face (if feminine) is not dankly glittering with perfumed mutton tallow (cold cream). You are a highly civilized couple, in bed at last after a toilsome day. Hurrah!

Hold that cheer. It would be a grand thing if you could now yield to that enchanted unconsciousness which all the poets recommend. "O magic Sleep!" wrote Keats; and again: "O soft embalmer of the still midnight, shutting, with careful fingers and benign, our gloom-pleased eyes!" John Milton had already written of "the dewy-feathered sleep" and Shakespeare of "the honey-heavy dew of slumber."

But this honey-heavy dew will not come regularly to you until you have faced Seven Great Problems, at least two of which have so far defied all human ingenuity. Science has no solution for them. Perhaps if you can suggest a universal remedy, your name will go on history's roll of honour with Edison and Pasteur.

29

Here are the problems:

1. In What Sort of Bed will you Sleep?

It has been settled that most people like the comradeship of sharing a room. It is far from settled that they like the comradeship of sharing a bed. Crowned heads of old solved this problem nicely. Either they snuggled together into a state bed about as big as a small battleship, or else they flouted comradeship by having separate apartments on different floors of their various palaces. But your home may not be a palace. You may be a bit cramped for separate apartments so long as your mother-in-law, your Aunt Mary, and her three lively children are making such a nice, long, indefinite visit to you.

So, for your cosy conjugal bedroom you will have to choose between twin beds or a double bed. Women are said to prefer the double bed, on the ground that they are more afraid of the dark than men, and "naturally prefer the comforting proximity of a bedfellow."

We are here quoting a high authority. He goes on to say that women know that twin beds cost twice as much to buy as double beds, and also twice as much in bedclothes and laundry. Or darned near it. Twin beds also take up one and a half times as much space as double beds. In spite of these objections, they are selling much, much faster than double beds.

It seems, then, that the average husband is not "comforting" as a bedfellow. His "proximity" is very likely an affair of loud snores, of throwing his arms and legs about as he sleeps, and of grabbing the blankets off his spouse and winding them round

The average husband is not comforting as a bedfellow.

himself like a cocoon. We shall discuss the cures for these disorders in their proper place. Meanwhile, there is just one safe rule in buying a double bed. Buy it big. The biggest we have found on the London market is sixty-three by seventy-six inches, which is no real Jumbo of a bed, but is still far better than the ordinary "double," in which you feel as if you were in a couple of bus seats, if not in a bureau drawer.

2. The Problem of Light

Is your room-mate or bed-mate a reader? Then he or she will want to pursue this hobby in bed. Only three years ago we thought this problem was insoluble by science. And lo! science has realized that the one who is trying to sleep is insufferably annoyed by the wide-spreading light of the bedfellow who loves to read. You can now buy what we called upon scientists to produce – a sort of electric spotlight that projects a beam of light directly on the book, and nowhere else.

Humanity has been fairly bellowing for such a gadget. If inventors had hurried up with it, instead of frittering away their time on things people didn't know they wanted – the telephone, for instance, or the self-starter for motor-cars – innumerable divorces might have been saved.

The problem of morning light is more difficult. You can shut it nicely out, as your ancestors did, by sleeping with the windows shut and the blinds tightly drawn. If, on the other hand, you love fresh air so much that you sleep on the upstairs verandah, you can buy a sort of burglar's mask that will exclude the light – and that may even exclude a burglar, by making him think that a fellow craftsman got up there before he did.

3. The Problem of Ventilation

Although this goes hand in hand with the problem of light, it really requires a bit of independent research and mutual flattery before you can settle it. It is a strange fact in all railway travelling, and in the operation of buses, stores, theatres, etc., that a person who loathes fresh air always prevails over a person who likes it. You are sitting in a stuffy, overheated railway carriage. Finally you lose your temper and open a window. Instantly your neighbour slams it down. If you venture to disagree, he calls the guard to enforce his wishes. Guards are always on the side of the majority; and the majority is terribly afraid of coolness, and even more afraid of draughts.

Before marriage, therefore, it is a useful thing to know if your intended feels about fresh air as you do. Argument won't help. Everybody has an unconscious memory of those centuries when it was universally thought that "the night air is poisonous." Our grandsires nailed their windows shut every autumn, and stuffed cotton wool into cracks in the window frames. Draughts were considered deadlier than daggers. If you have broken the human race's inherited dread of fresh air, be sure to marry somebody who thinks as you do. Otherwise, until air-conditioning arrives everywhere – and enables you to do surreptitious things with a little valve after your consort is asleep – you will disagree every night. To you, the breeze from the open window seems assurance of health and repose. To your bedfellow, it is merely a proof that you want to bring the rigours of the Arctic into the room.

4. The Unsolved Problem of Noise

Mayors proclaim against noise. There are dreadful penalties in London and other cities for tooting your horn after bedtime. Motor lorries backfire. Firemen love to zoom through the streets with their sirens shrieking. The roar and clatter of the traffic is London's familiar lullaby. We know a noise more destructive to connubial felicity than any of these things. It is the common snore.

This is the first of the two great nocturnal problems that haven't yielded to science, although science – having invested years of time on such baubles as the alternating current – is now taking up snoring in a serious way. It seems to be definitely proved that only contented people snore. Their facial muscles relax, their mouths open. The mouth must be wide open before snoring can be done loudly and efficiently. So one remedy is to make your bedfellow a bit less contented with his or her lot. If recent business conditions, starting about 1929, haven't done this, the chances are that nothing can do it.

The mouth must be wide open before snoring can be done loudly and efficiently.

The next remedy is a chin strap. This is on the market, and it does keep the mouth closed. Unfortunately, no snorer is ever absolutely persuaded that he or she is guilty. It is far easier to assume that one is being traduced, maligned and insulted. So in presenting a chin strap to your bedfellow, if you have enough courage to do it, you might suggest that it is an adjunct to beauty – a preserver of the contours of the throat and jaw, a preventive of double chin.

Unhappily, any person vain enough to fall for this good selling point in favour of the chin strap will be quite vain enough to study its appearance in the mirror. This appearance is not good. Even the handsomest horse loses grace and charm when his nose-bag is adjusted, and the result of wearing a chin strap is much the same.

So the last resort is to plug up your own ears. Oddly, most people fail hopelessly at this. They use absorbent cotton wool, which is a good conductor of sound. It may keep water out of your ears when you are swimming, but it won't keep snoring out. Rubber is also no sound-proofer. What is on the market now, in the form of ear-plugs, are little gadgets made of wax and cotton, which are but partially effective. Even so, trying to plug your own ears is a palliative – but not a cure. If the snorer is contented enough to sleep through a fire-alarm, and if you are sound-proofed enough to sleep through it too – why, you might both be burned in your bed. Or to think of something less disagreeable, you might miss a midnight telephone call from a lawyer in Australia, who is trying to tell you that you have inherited a fortune.

5. The Problem of Pillows

This is, comparatively, a trifle. Men like their pillows harder and more numerous than women do. Lie right down on the pillow counter in the shop, if need be, and make sure. Get your bedfellow to lie down in turn. You may give the gentlemanly shopwalker a few hearty laughs, but your head is going to be on a pillow for a third of your remaining lifetime. Why not test the pillow almost as carefully as you would test a pair of shoes, or anything else which you buy? Pillows do come in various shapes, sizes, and degrees of softness. You can get what you like.

6. The Problem of Waking Up

This is vexatious. It springs from the fact that we all sleep with varying intensities. Some do their heaviest sleeping early, some late. King George V is said to have solved the little problem of royal punctuality by keeping all the palace clocks half an hour fast. You can possibly do this, and fool yourself enough to catch the 8.5 at least one day a week. But you can't fool any bedfellow in the world into waking up naturally just when you do. And you can't find an alarm clock that will wake a heavy sleeper without also arousing a light one. So you will just have to reconcile yourself to a little unpleasantness every morning, and smooth it over all you can with fair words.

7. The Problem of Warmth

This is the terrible problem, the enigma from which our baffled scientists reel away in despair. Given two people in two different rooms, there is no problem. One can shiver under six blankets and two eiderdowns. The other, on the same night, will be gasping for air under nothing but a sheet. Each is happy after his or her own fashion.

Put those people into twin beds, and the problem is still not unconquerable. The shivery one can wear bed-socks, and use a hot-water bottle, and wear flannel pyjamas, and have as many blankets, etc., as he pleases. The warm-blooded one can go the limit in stripping the bed and herself (or himself, as the case may be).

But now put these people into a double bed.

Absolutely no blankets have ever been made that will stay over one sleeper, and not over the other. Diagonal folds are of no use. Half-sized blankets slip off you. Finally you have to compromise the whole matter. The shivery bedfellow pulls a lot of bedclothes over both the parties. The warm-blooded one presently kicks them off again. This is exactly the sort of thing that makes war between nations. It makes the Thirty Years' War look like a week-end when it starts in a married couple's life. We have no remedy.

There is one thing that helps the shivery combatant a great deal, and that is a realization that a whole lot of warmth went out of the world with the old-fashioned feather bed. When you slept on one of those, you were warm. In fact, you soon came very nearly to a boil. That is because feathers are a fine insulator. Unhappily, cold-blooded people have given up feather beds, and now sleep on mattresses full of spiral springs. It keeps you just as cold as if you were sleeping on the floor. Colder. It pumps the chilly air against you, as you stir in your sleep. Piling bedclothes on top of you is no good. Well, it is some good. But not enough.

But as we said, science hasn't solved the problem of how two people can gratify their own individual ideas of necessary warmth in a double bed. The largest manufacturer of beds in this country says gloomily that he doesn't think science ever will. But we think that the double bed of the future – when Utopia comes – will be marked H on one side and C on the other, like your bath taps. How the Utopians will achieve this we don't know. They will do it somehow – perhaps on the very day they learn how to abolish war, to extract gold from sea water, and to cure a common cold.

THE SEVEN PILLARS OF
DESERTION AND DIVORCE

1. An all-night mosquito hunt, in which you step several times on your sleeping partner's abdomen.

2. Any nocturnal conversation concerning lack of money in your family.

3. Permanently cold feet.

4. Cold cream and curling pins.

5. Pyjama pants that don't match the jacket.

6. Any dentifrice flavoured with wintergreen.

7. The lack of any dentifrice at all.

3

How to Go to Bed

THIS chapter is for the conjugal couple alone. Others may skip. We are not suggesting that you will skip for joy because you are not one half a conjugal couple. If you are alone, however, and go to bed with no human eye upon you except that of a dormitory master, a house mistress or some such person, you can dispense with ordinary politeness. Just fall into bed the best way you can.

But are you a wife? Then you have been exasperated all day by house-to-house salesmen, and by tradespeople. Your bridge game may not have been prosperous. Your motor-car drive may have been harassed by reckless policemen. When your husband came home, you may have had to break the news to him that he was expected to take your mother and yourself to dinner and an evening of chamber music at the Whiffenpoofs – whom he abhors. You have come at last to the final stages of mutual exasperation. You are the martyr of the party, but your husband looks as if he were standing heroically at the stake. Very well. Here is your chance to give him a real surprise.

Instead of leaping out and finding your way at once with the electric torch to your back door, your can stand patiently while he shuts the garage doors. When you are both safely in the kitchen, it is time for a stupefying remark. Here is a good one, warranted to delight the surliest male. Say: "Wouldn't you like a whisky-and-soda before going to bed?"

At this point, your mother will be so appalled that she will hurry upstairs, leaving her son-in-law to his horrid orgy. Surely, the glass of sherry served by the Whiffenpoofs before dinner should be enough for any man who wants to keep his head clear for next day.

But it isn't enough. After a moment of surprise, your husband will look at you and say: "Why, yes   I really hadn't thought of it, but I would like a drop of whisky very much indeed."

All this time, you have stood convincingly by the sideboard, with the sort of expression which Circe donned when receiving her well-known visitors. Of course, you are not really going to turn your husband into a swine. If he is a teetotaller, you can easily substitute his usual total of tea. Otherwise, take out of the refrigerator a bottle of soda water, extract some ice cubes from their chilly little coffin, place them in a bowl, arrange some cigarettes, biscuits and cheese on a tray, and have everything ready when your husband wanders back with the whisky bottle. He will then sit down and enjoy himself. If the cat happens to be mewing around, and looks prepared to put up a stiff argument before he is thrust outdoors, do the thrusting yourself while your husband quaffs.

Then is time for stupefying remark number two. Say: "Make yourself comfortable – I'll see that everything is shut up for the night." While this remark is producing its effect, you can nimbly return all the supplies to their place and put the bottle back in its cupboard. As soon as you have entered your bedroom, assure yourself that your husband's bed (if a twin) is turned down, and that his nightclothes and slippers are neatly laid out on it. Then slip into your best-looking nightie or pyjamas, leave the bathroom in that almost surgically spick-and-span condition which men demand at their clubs, and await the reaction.

This reaction may not be immediate. It takes some time for any idea to penetrate any masculine intelligence. But sooner or later, a husband treated by his wife as he would expect to be treated by even the least capable house man will say: "I have managed to keep about two hundred pounds away from the creditors – and you not only want a new evening gown but we both need a little cruise to Bermuda or somewhere."

All of which is a proof that men are not so unobservant and indifferent as they seem. The very same man who drove home in a cloud of sullen boredom, wondering aloud why people are willing to annoy themselves with fussy food and meaningless music, may under these deft manipulations prove as charming a room-mate to you as he was to the boys at school. One whisky-and-soda on retiring – or any other potation, from brandy to buttermilk – makes the average man forget the dullest dinner and sends him to bed in a glow of good will. He will be still more amiable if, when he starts to brush his teeth, he does not find your gloves soaking in the wash-basin and looking like a nest of very cold pickled eels.

Now, are you a husband? Have you learned to retire without preliminary discord? What are perfect going-to-bed manners for you? This problem is not so simple as it seems. Your technique is something like that we have outlined for your wife, but it must be far more subtle. Otherwise she will think you are just playing a part.

Do not over-act. It may produce sudden domestic harmony, after years of connubial squalls, if you merely start wearing clean pyjamas every night. You might even, very cautiously, take a bath before turning in. The spectacle of a thoroughly clean man, dressed in spotless clothes, is just as pleasing to a normal female at bedtime as it is at lunch – or any other time. The man who comes lurching up to bed from the billiard-room, with chalk on his face and cigar ashes in his finger-nails, will be all the better for a good wash. And if his evening has been a long one, he will be all the better for a shave.

This is a terrific reform, far too radical for the ordinary man. Shaving in the morning is a ritual. It doesn't matter if the water is cold, if the only new packet of blades has been lost, if the hand is unsteady after too few hours of sleep – the average business man has it deeply ingrained in his sense of propriety that he must shave before he goes to the office. At night he could do a leisurely, even artistic, job. But no. He is determined to present a freshly shaved face to the people on the platform, to the ticket collector, to the crowd on the Underground, and to the office boy who is distributing his letters. The fact that he presented his stubbly jowls to his wife, at bedtime, is of no importance to him. That is what wives are for.

It will please your wife, however, if you can manage to get to bed without encrusting her toilet soap and hair brushes with cigarette ashes. It will also please her if some night you can forget to wonder audibly why a woman wants a filthy cat around the house. It will enravish her if you make even a feeble effort, off your own bat, to fix the window blind which has been balky for a year.

But again – don't over-act! Do these things naturally. Let them happen the way a glacier moves. Slowly, slowly! If you reform completely some night, it will sow the seeds of enduring suspicion. Your wife thinks of you exactly as modern hospital attendants think of their mental patients. Never will she believe that you have all your buttons. You are to be condoned, if not applauded, for undressing by gravity. (This consists in unfastening your lower garments at the waist, and letting them all sink on to the floor. If you are very neat, you probably then give them a place-kick on to a chair.) Your wife picks up after you more than you think, and smiles without rancour as she picks your pipe out of the butter-dish, when you have sprinted out of the door to catch that 8.25 train.

So it will never, never do to remodel your bed manners overnight. Your wife's idea of a really attractive man is that Woofwoofski fellow, who played the violin at the concert. He spent all the afternoon, probably, having his nails polished – while you, in the seven minutes you had to dress after coming home, couldn't even find your nail file. Never mind. Your wife was there in the pinch with an orange stick. She understands more than you think about the heroic, almost uncomplaining, rush in which your days are spent. Don't compete with the fiddler-man. Let him have the field to himself.

But this advice doesn't mean that you can relapse entirely into grateful barbarism. You are probably snorting with indignation at the idea that it might pay to hang up your clothes neatly, and even to take a bath, and even to shave. As for fixing the window blind, what do we think you are? A mechanic? No. We doubt if you are mechanical enough to do it, sir.

But we have suggested some ideas which can charm and even enslave the most unreasonable of women. If your night life at present is a sort of war of attrition, with both sides grimly holding on to their positions, you may accomplish much with a few strokes of strategy. In time of war, why not prepare for peace?

GETTING UNDRESSED

If you were sentenced to spend nine years of your life working at one job for eight hours a day – Sundays included – you would think harshly of the judge. Statistics prove, however, that the average man, with a life span of seventy years, spends this amount of time taking off his clothes and putting them on again.[1] The amount of time similarly spent by the average woman can be measured only in light-years.

Being condemned to this slavery from birth, one would think people would learn how to do the job with a little finesse. To most people undressing is not so much an art as it is a coming to pieces.

This is a mistake. Failure to correct it has been responsible for the development of a good-sized city in the western hemisphere, composed of exiled husbands. If the average ignorant bird should hurl his feathers around the nest each night in imitation of man, there would be no more eggs.

Some of the principal sins against good breeding are committed in the process of removing the clothes. In putting them on most people are conferring such a

---

1 These figures do not include nudists, Esquimos, bedridden people or dancers.

Coming to pieces.

favour on the sensitive eye that lapses of etiquette are more pardonable. Whatever you do, avoid the habit of getting undressed by gravity. The appearance of puddles of male or female clothing on the bedroom floor never caused a tremor of love in the most sensitive bosom. Our researches show that women are particularly prone to this moult-and-walk-off process. They have one strange garment they call a step-in. All of them might be called step-outs. They also have a rubber fabric strait-jacket called a vassarette. Getting into it is a job for a contortionist. Getting out of it is a bit easier, if your grandmother was a snake and you have inherited the knack of shedding your skin.

Most men are partly sloppy undressers. One group practises what is known professionally as the drop-kick. This consists of allowing the sub-waist clothing to slide down the legs, lifting one foot out of the resulting nest, and propelling the entire mass at the nearest chair with the toe. Avoid it. An even larger school spends futile years throwing odds and ends of clothes at bedrooms chairs. These men argue that bedroom chairs serve no other useful purpose. No one has ever been known to sit on them. We advise against it, however, even if it is done in the purest spirit of sportsmanship.

Regardless of how clothes may be worn they should be taken off unostentatiously. Once off, they should not be treated like Christmas tree decorations. Get them out of sight. Far better to shove them under the bed with the foot than to wake up each morning to the sordid contemplation of their wilted forms. The seeds of many fashionable divorces have been sown by these early-morning vistas. What man can shave with a loving heart while contemplating a bedrabbled brassière hanging on the bathroom rail? What woman, lying in bed because it is too cold to get up, has not wondered sadly how the handsome lad of yesterday can possibly fill out a pair of pants like that?

This brings us to the question of getting dressed, which is so buttoned up with a number of other things that we will treat it somewhere else, if the matter should come up.

IN BED

Face it frankly. In bed you were born, in bed you will die. Just as if these two experiences didn't teach you anything, you now purpose in cold blood to spend thirty-three and one-third per cent of all your time in bed – and, if you are not married already, you expect to induce some fellow creature to share bed's dangers with you. This you do because you can't help it. The instinct is inherited. Don't be ashamed of it.

The moose is a land animal, the monkey a tree animal, the whale a water animal. But man is a bed animal, and the only one in the world (except woman, of course). Considering how fond she is of breakfasting in bed, and of "lying down" on the bed in spare hours, woman is even more of a bed animal than man. Admitting this fact, the authors have tried to show you how to get into bed as gracefully as possible. If you are unmarried it really doesn't much matter if you hurl your clothes about the room, or festoon them on bureaus and chairs. They offend no eye but your own, while you're in bed. In the morning, after you are out, some humble servitor like your chambermaid, your valet, or your mother, will pick up after you.

In the same way, if you have no bedfellow you can be as sloppy as you like in bed. You can use the sheet for a handkerchief. You can put your muddy boots on the bedspread, when snoozing before dinner. You can drink whisky out of the bottle, spilling some of it on the pillow case. You can burn holes in the blankets with cigarettes. These social errors don't matter except to the menial – be it laundress or mother – who does your wash and your mending. Try any of these tricks on a bedfellow, however, and you will find yourself out of luck. It is best to wean yourself of all of them before you ask for a marriage licence. Otherwise you will always look back on your wedding night as the night of the Big Blizzard.

PRETTY COSTUMES FOR BED

The first great rule is: Wear correct clothes in bed, or none at all. Our ancestors either went to bed with all their clothes on, or else they went to bed raw. Good breeding now decrees the use of nice-looking nightgowns and pyjamas. Women are allowed to choose between these articles. Men have no choice. It is pyjamas for them or nothing.

The comfortable old-fashioned flannel nightgown, worn with bed socks, is taboo

So is the practice, common among seamen and lumberjacks, of going to bed in one's underclothes. A man who does this in the nuptial chamber is crude. This is especially true if you actually are a lumberjack, in which case you wear long woollen drawers, and an undershirt with long sleeves, both made of heavy grey or red knitted goods.

The eye of a sensitive, delicately reared girl is shocked by such an inartistic sleeping costume. It is your own fault if she screams. You should be wearing a Japanese brocade dressing-gown over silk pyjamas. Lumberjacks who do this make good husbands. So do other men. Socks are not being worn in bed this year. The whole art of dressing for bed, in fact, is not to wear anything that could irritate your bolster-buddy or counterpane-chum, call her whatever you will. It is true that "misery makes strange bedfellows," as the proverb says. It is even more true that bedfellows make strange misery – unless they are determined in advance to be nice to one another at all costs.

ETIQUETTE WHILE HORIZONTAL

It is quite easy to show good manners while you are vertical. This is the normal position when taking off your hat to a lady, or selling her a bottle of gin in a shop, or any other civilized action. When you assume a horizontal position, however, whole centuries of traditional good breeding disappear. This is the moment which ordinary writers about etiquette never discuss. They seem to think you are vertical all the time. Standing up, or sitting up. This is nonsense, as we have just proved by showing you that you want to be horizontal so much of your life.

We now answer a few ordinary questions, which everybody wants to ask, but which the authorities have never answered before.

Q. Which goes to bed first, a wife or her husband?

A. The wife who beats her husband at getting into bed leaves him to open the window, adjust the shade, and take a last look at the heating apparatus. If she has good sense, she will win this race every night.

Q. Who gets up if there is a noise like burglars?

A. Nobody.

Q. What are fashionable topics to discuss in bed?

A. The morals, or lack of morals, of your neighbours; the wretched food and drink served at their houses; the bad manners of their children. These are all safe and reliable themes.

Q. Are any topics barred by good manners?

A. Yes. Avoid all discussion of money-worries, of your own morals (or lack of them), of the quality of food and drink served in your own home, and the manners of your own children. All these are dynamite.

Q. What does a husband do if the wife is sure the house is on fire?

A. He argues with her till morning, if necessary, taking the negative side of the debate. If he gets up to investigate, there is always the chance that she may be right.

Important as all these items are, they are nothing compared to the face cream and hair curler problem. This is the biggest question of the day – excuse us, we mean the night. It cannot be dismissed briefly. It dwarfs even the snoring problem; and the halitosis problem beside it is a pygmy.

All women have been taught, in the past fifteen years, that it is fatal to let the hair and the skin alone. The hair must be curled. The skin of the face must be covered with cold cream. If these things aren't done just as regularly as the sun sets, a woman loses her membership card in her own sex. She can't even tell you what would happen if she failed just once in this ritual. It is more than a ritual to her. It is a creed.

The average man, we are glad to say, marries a pretty girl. Prettiness and daintiness are the things he values. He remembers Milton's line about some lucky chap who spent a lot of time "lost in the tangles of Neaera's hair" – Neaera being the prettiest nymph of her day and age. The average man also enjoys the advertisements about that schoolgirl complexion. He adores a soft pink cheek. And what happens to him?

On tiptoe with expectancy, he finds himself at last alone, behind locked doors, with the pretty girl of his choice. He is on his best behaviour. He has used the right soap, the right mouthwash, the right toothpaste, and the right liniment to cure all the unpleasant symptoms mentioned in the other advertisements he reads. He has fixed his hair brilliantly. He has bought a lovely silk dressing gown and pyjamas. His feet are in costly slippers. He feels and looks on the crest of the wave. His bride, at this moment, comes out of the bathroom.

How to Go to Bed

The shock to a sensitive man's feelings, which now occurs, is likely to send him to a lunatic asylum for life.

The bride's head is covered with a network of large, shiny wire gadgets, resembling safety pins, much enlarged. They pull her hair so hard that her eyes are all squinched up. This alters her expression so much that he doesn't at first recognize her. She is wearing a pretty peignoir, over a new pink night-gown – the costliest in her trousseau. But he doesn't even see these things. His eyes travel down from her hair to her face. And her face is like a leper's, as white as snow.

When the first shock passes, he realizes that this is the way she is going to look to him every night of their lives. He has heard about curlers and cream. But until he marries, no woman has dared to show them to him. His mother, his sisters, etc., have been too anxious to preserve his good opinion. His wife, on the other hand, feels free from the start to behave naturally.

That same night, some lawyer in Reno is ordering a case of expensive champagne. He knows he can afford it all right. Members of the legal fraternity, out there, are assured of living on the fat of the land as long as curlers and cream are made and wives allowed to buy them. This is where divorces begin.

YOUR KNIGHT LIFE HAS ITS PERILS

Even if the wife is be-wired and be-whitened, however, and the husband has hung up all his good manners in the cupboard with his clothes, the nights have to be lived through, somehow. The best plan is to say very little.

We have outlined a few harmless topics, which are fun for both persons. Still, almost any chatter can lead, before you know it, to a hail of abuse like machine-gun fire. Any mention of money is an extra-hazardous occupation. Having settled the neighbours' hash with a few well chosen remarks, you should quickly steer the conversation to art, literature, or politics. This will soon put your pillow-pal to sleep. You can now cautiously doze off yourself, taking great pains not to snore. If you snore like the foghorn of an ocean steamer, your mattress-mate will wake up, and all's to do over again.

Never despair, however. Practice makes perfect in knight life, as in everything else. Avoid mumbling and talking in your sleep. This is discourteous, and it may also be too interesting to the hearer. Do not walk in your sleep. Getting up to do this admits a blast of cold air into the bed which will cause discomfort to your bedfellow.

Do not grind your teeth in your sleep, or toss and twist so much that you wind the bedclothes into a tight cocoon around yourself, leaving your pillow-partner bare. Try to turn off the radio at an early moment after midnight. All these things require some self-denial, but remember what Emerson said. "Good manners," he said, "are made up of petty sacrifices."

HOW TO INVITE SOMEBODY TO BED

You "date yourself" far more by what you say than by the way you look. The use of worn-out language (especially slanguage) is fatal to the best efforts of your barber and tailor, your gymnasium instructor, and all the others who try to make you seem youthful and sprightly. And if you're a lady – why, you may spend your allowance ten times over at the dressmaker's and the beauty parlour, and still be recognized for a grandmother if you use a grandmother's wise-cracks.

If you say:
"Let us retire!" you date from the 1870's.

If you say:
"Let's hit the hay!" you date from the 1880's.

If you speak of your bed as "the feathers," you are using slang of nearly as ancient vintage. To speak of going to bed as "flopping" is also not very new. In fact there is nothing safer and more modern to say than "Let's go to bed."

But people do get tired of saying this over and over again, especially if they have to say it several times every evening, before good results are attained. Comical bishops in novels usually vary it by making up a phrase such as "Let's all go to Bedfordshire!" But this also is old. To be thought young and dashing you need a wholly new piece of slang. It is always piquant to make it up yourself, and not depend on seeing it in the newspaper, or overhearing it at a party. Here is the way to proceed:

It was funny to call a bed "the hay" for a few years after the mattress was stuffed with hay. But your mattress is now stuffed with selected horsehair, full of correctly tempered hour-glass springs, and magically insulated with fleecy felt. If you don't believe us, cut it open. Or read the advertisement of that mattress.

You would surprise and perhaps charm almost anybody, even your husband, if instead of saying "Let's hit the hay!" you said: "Let's hit the selected horsehair, full of correctly tempered hourglass springs, etc., etc." But maybe this is too long to learn by heart – and it certainly won't sound funny twice.

What you need, to refresh your way of speaking, are some good, reliable words that mean "bed." A short list includes bunk, berth, pallet, crib, cot, shakedown, lit (French) and palang (Hindu). Then you want a few good words that mean "lie down," "yawn," "snore," "take a rest," and so forth. You might trust the dictionary, but never trust a dictionary too far. Or you will find yourself saying to some startled person, who never went to a classical school, something that he or she won't understand.

Only if your wife went to Somerville can you say:

"I am somniferous. Are you statuvolvent? Shall we oscitate in our palang?"

It is really simpler to say:

"Let's go to bed".

A WOMAN'S BEST FRIEND IS
HER HOT-WATER BOTTLE

One bedfellow that never loses charm for any woman is her hot-water bottle.

Inventors have burst upon the modern scenes with electric warming pads, and with gadgets which you can plunge into hot water and which are guaranteed to stay hot for hours. We are not talking of these things.

We are talking of the common or chemists'-shop hot-water bottle, invented in 1873 by a man named Reuben Fuzzletisch. You can buy it anywhere. It may be still the 1873 model. It may grow old and decrepit in your service. Its screw top may be leaky. It may look as if it were going to burst at any minute. No matter. The woman who has become dependent on it will cherish it to the end.

All through that last dismal, sleepy rubber of bridge at the Spoopendykes' house, with the cold draught simply roaring across the floor and chilling her feet, her eye will brighten when she thinks of the faithful hot-water bottle hanging on its bathroom hook at home. Though she is far too tired to join you in the midnight snack recommended on an earlier page of this book, she is not too tired to get the bottle and light the heater, or put the kettle on the stove. Filling her nocturnal hotwater bottle is a rite that outlasts her prayers, her faith in the League of Nations, and all her other most cherished little credos.

One of the nastiest nocturnal adventures…

Watch her as she puts the bottle into her bed and adjusts its genial, faintly gurgling shape to her chilly feet. Watch her as she shifts it to other suffering parts of her anatomy. You will wonder why men have erected statues to the man who invented nothing more ingratiating than the sewing machine. Why, if we hadn't told you the name of Mr. Fuzzletisch you wouldn't have felt so strongly moved to subscribe for a statue to him.

If you are a man, and it falls to your lot to share a bed with a woman and a hot-water bottle, don't try to get it away from her. Any violent grabbing with your hands, or soccer football tactics with your feet, will burst it. This is one of the nastiest nocturnal adventures that can happen.

A man's best friend is his dog. But don't encourage your dog to think he's going to maintain his position on your bed after you marry. The snores, the scratching and shifting and also the aroma of your four-footed bedmate will be something to conceal from an innocent bride. You may possibly solve this problem by inducing good Towser to go and get married himself.

SO YOU DON'T SLEEP WELL!

Now tiptoe with us to the bedroom of any person who sleeps badly. Watch this person prepare for a night's repose. All through the evening, he told you he was a martyr to insomnia. Eyes gleaming dewily with self-pity, he assured you that he never gets a good night's rest. Every night is a sleepless night for him. And why not? He sets up everything for it.

Beside his bed is a large table, and on the table you notice a lamp, a water jug, a glass, a teaspoon, a packet of bromides, an assortment of other powders and pills, a plate of fruit, a box of cigarettes, a wireless, some cotton wool to put in his ears, a black bandage to tie over his eyes before sunrise, a bottle of whisky, a manicure set, a pack of cards, a thermometer, and a couple of detective stories. Just about what a man would need to keep him amused and interested through an Arctic night. But is our friend amused? Not he.

So our friend is a victim not only of insomnia, and wishes he could have his bedroom fully sound-proofed. If very rich, he has done so. The effect is sepulchral. You feel that in this tomb-like room, the wings of a single mosquito would thunder like an aeroplane motor. But the "victim" is gloomily hopeful

Bed Manners

that the sound-proofing will exclude the chirps of early morning sparrows, and the snorts of the milkman's horse. Let's leave him to his fun. The bedside table of his will keep him fully occupied all night. Never a dull moment!

One method is called psychiatry. You can either pay several guineas a week for it, or try it without any expense at home. Suppose you do try, and fail. Where are you going to get eighteen holes of golf in London? Are you going to tee your ball on the Club door-step, and see how many strokes it will take you to reach Wimbledon? You would be arrested. Where are you going to get a loom, and what would your boss say if you started to work it in the office? Good bed manners and good sense require, if you do have insomnia, to have it privately and not wake up the whole household. Worry and insufficient exercise cause it. The sharpest attacks come on the nights before you are going to fight some battle of Waterloo in the office, or when you just can't meet your overdraft at the bank.

You will wonder, after a few hours, why you ever were able to sleep. You will hear the traffic throbbing and roaring, as loudly as it ever does in daytime. To your aching ears it will sound louder. Your pillow will feel like a washboard. Your bedclothes will stick to you in clammy corrugations. No position is

68

comfortable. All the rest of you aches, as well as your ears. Steady now. If you go down and look for cigarettes, every floor board will creak under your feet. You may trip over the cat. Yet you can't stay in bed. Yes, you can read a little – it will tire your eyes and make you sleep.

So you pick up the latest by Phillips Oppenheim. This author lives by making his customers gasp, by curdling their blood, by setting their hearts to pounding. When you get to the place where the international opium smugglers have Lady Geraldine Maltravers in their hellish power – and where only one man in Europe has the power to save her, and he is on his way in heavy irons to Devil's Island – why, when you get to that comparatively mild situation in the story, you will be beyond the aid of any sedative. But you probably will put the book down, and take a sedative. If it wouldn't wake the family, you would turn on the wireless. You do throttle it down and turn it on. Lively dance tunes. Lively police messages. You wish some intelligent announcer would say: "You will now receive eight hours of silence."

Nobody does. You turn off the entertainment. Phillips Oppenheim and the sedative are still struggling furiously inside you. You moodily go over, for the eighty-fifth time, the little speech you are going to make at the bank – or the little speech that you didn't make to Mr. Higgenbottom at the office, when he said that your services were required no longer. You're in for it. If you tiptoe to the sideboard for an orange, you'll wake up your mother. You're too tired to get up. Too tired to stay in bed. Getting up is the lesser of these two evils – but you'll have to get up and get out, to work a real cure.

Don't put on a dressing-gown and prowl around the house until everybody is awake and either cursing or consoling you after their fashion. Get up, dress, and go out. There is one chance in a million, of course, that you will be robbed by a highwayman. But the fact is that you will seem to be a highwayman yourself. Innocent passers-by will shrink away from you as you swing along, with your hat down over your eyes.

What a busy place London is at night. Even the side streets. What lots of people are always up. What lots of all-night restaurants. After five miles or so, at a swinging clip, a hot dog tastes pretty good, a cup of coffee is nectar.

Gosh, you shouldn't have taken that coffee! It will only keep you awake. But you are interested in the pink dawn behind the tall buildings, now you're seeing it at your ease on a park bench, and not out of a taxicab window. It's exciting. If you weren't so terribly sleepy at this point... If you weren't all tired out by hitting the hard pavements... You're yawning right in the face of the copper who is looking so hard at you. Oh, take a taxi and go home to bed.

This radical cure for insomnia is recommended only to gentlemen. It turns them into either excellent sleepers or competent night prowlers – two very good methods of passing the time. We do not think a lady should walk the streets at night. She can solve her problem by reading some suitable book – not a mystery story – but one of the great, admired, educational masterpieces, which will soothe her and instruct her, too. Don't try to tell us you haven't such a book. What's that in your hand now?

4

On Coming Home Late

COMING HOME FROM STAG DINNERS

IF you must come home at an ungodly hour from little dinners, the best way is not to come home at all. Sometimes, however, you may not discover what a spirited little dinner you have let yourself in for until it is too late. When discretion gives the whispered suggestion that perhaps you'd better spend the night in town, curb your first hot impulse to phone the little woman and tell her all about it frankly.

Go to the telephone booth. Hold the receiver hook down with your finger. Repeat your message aloud several times. If you cannot understand it yourself, have a flunkey come and listen to you. If he cannot understand it, go back to the dinner and have a good time. Nothing that can happen to you now will be as bad as what you have just missed.

Hours later, your feet will crunch the gravel of your suburban drive. It is life's darkest moment. Keep your head. Remember that knowledge is power. As you enter your conjugal nest, do not be deceived by the sweet little form which appears to slumber there so innocently. That sheeted form is not slumbering. It has been lying awake since midnight, visualizing your mangled body scattered along the public highway.

That sheeted form is not slumbering.

Experience should teach us many things. When competing with hope, however, it always loses. Above all, do not let the knowledge of woman's maternal instinct lull you into a prodigal-son complex. As your erring foot stumbled across the threshold, love, the yellow little cur, flew out of the window. It is a moment when the fatted calf is the one and only thing your wife is not prepared to kill.

The best thing is to avoid the bedroom as if it were a contagious ward. Disrobe as quietly as possible in any other part of the house. Kick your clothes into a corner. The maid will sneak them up for you in the morning. Then try to reach the bed without turning on the light. Of course, by doing this you are robbing your mate of much innocent amusement. Statistics indicate, however, that in such situations it is smart to be selfish. Should you trip up in the dark and fall heavily you can always blame it upon a carelessly placed chair. Or, if you are in a bold mood, you can lie in your own blood for an hour or two, hoping that she will conclude that you fell into bed and, thus comforted, go to sleep and forget about it.

You may be foiled, however, by a night light left burning beside your bed. If so, carefully avoid all attempts to be light and dainty in your movements.

Hostile eyes are upon you whenever your back is turned. Many a well-planned undressing effort has been ruined by boastfully trying to stand on one foot and remove a sock. There is nothing more treacherous and unfriendly than a sock. Just when it appears to be slipping off like a snake skin, and you are prepared to let your upheld foot fall to the floor where it belongs, the miserable thing suddenly grips your heel like an octopus. Unless you are quick, you will find yourself tangled in a horrid mess in a corner of the bedroom. Far safer to sit in a dignified manner on the edge of the bed and approach things methodically.

Another form of self-display which has had unfortunate results is reaching. Play safe. Keep your desires as simple as possible. If you must have something, however, don't reach for it. Walk to it. A failure can become historic.

There is one cardinal rule in connection with entering the bedroom under these conditions. Surprisingly enough, it is frequently neglected. Before going into the house give yourself a thorough spiritual examination. If you discover the slightest impulse in your bosom to be kind and genial, tear it out as if it were a viper. Far better to go to the back of the house and have a few minutes' chat with the clothes post than allow this tendency to go indoors with you.

Sometimes these attacks of good fellowship are hard to detect, however, until it is too late. If this should happen, take pains to avoid an Oxford accent. No matter how perfect a picture you may paint of the wholesome dinner you have just attended, if you do it like an English professor with a cold in his head the results will be unsatisfactory.

Don't be discouraged if you have failures at the start. Some people have nothing else. They are what is technically known as bedroom-conscious. We knew of one case which developed this complex to such an extent that the patient couldn't come home from a Boy Scout rally without bursting into hiccoughs on the front stairs and measuring his length on the connubial threshold. It eventually ruined him. He found that he was in trouble no matter what he did, so he set out to get his money's worth. If you are afflicted in this way, we suggest that you change your job. Become a travelling salesman.

THE WIFE WHO STAYS OUT LATE

Modern women have emancipated themselves from the absurd old notion that "woman's place is in the home." Do you know why your ancestors wear such grim, strained expressions in the family photograph album? It is because they were always at home together. Never a respite, never a reprieve. As soon as work was over for the day, and a hearty twelve-course dinner eaten, they gathered around the parlour lamp and glared at each other until it was time to go to bed. In other words, until it was half-past nine o'clock. Civilization has ended this ghastly custom.

It has made it almost obligatory for a refined woman to belong to a culture class which meets on Monday evenings, a bridge club which meets on Tuesday evenings, a charity organization which meets on Wednesday evenings, and so on. This keeps her from staying at home and picking on her husband and the children.

Another agency which has helped to get Mother out of the house is science. To appreciate what science has done for women consider Nancy Hanks. Her housewifely duties consisted in getting up before dawn, taking care of the livestock, cooking breakfast, weeding the garden, picking and shelling peas, digging and peeling potatoes, helping to kill pigs, wringing chicken's necks, winding wool, making clothes, teaching the baby boy his letters, scrubbing floors, cooking dinner, making jam, etc. (This is only a partial list.) It suggests what you would be doing, gentle reader, if it weren't for such blessings as tinned soup and electric gadgets in every room.

The modern housewife has no work of any kind to do.[2] To keep her mind and muscles occupied, she has therefore handsomely paid Mr. Sims, Mr. Culbertson, and a few other brainy gentlemen to complicate the simple old game of whist for her, until it has become almost a life work to learn to play it. Instead of reading for herself, which on the authority of Dr. Charles W. Eliot takes "only fifteen minutes a day," she has formed clubs to take up hours and hours in the discussion of books, and the eating of salads.

All these things represent progress. If they don't fill your time, there is always charity. Martha Washington's idea of charity was to fill some baskets with good food, and take them directly to poor people. This is too simple and quick to be modern. You must

2 Dr Hopton wrote this chapter and wouldn't let me see it until too late to correct his nonsense.—ANNE BALLIOL.

now hold a lot of meetings, and elect officers, and give yourself and your fellow workers a banquet at the best hotel, and employ a press agent, and a professional money-raising firm, before the poor folks get so much as a chicken bone. If they ever do get it.

After self-improvement and charity, the most refined way to break the shackles of the home is motoring. Every discriminating woman now has her own car, or will have as soon as the motor-car manufacturers can spread the gospel. A car of her own will help immensely in keeping a housewife out

The lady will show similar good manners.

in God's great out-of-doors during the day. And often, far into the night.

The house husband of such a housewife is sure to be a quiet, domestic little chap, who loves to take his slippered ease at the fireside, and to go to bed early. He will generally be in bed before she comes home from the Family Welfare meeting. What is the correct etiquette for him when he hears her latchkey in the door? His first instinct as a gentleman, will be to get up, shout "Hello, my pretty one!" in a hearty voice, and then forage in the icebox for a nice midnight snack for her. His first instinct, as a husband, will be to say: "Who have you been out with to-night?" He must sternly repress both these instincts.

His wife will not be hungry. If she has been at a literary meeting, she will have partaken of a light buffet supper of cocktails, canapes, lobster patties, chicken salad, beer, ice-cream and cake. If she has been conferring with some gentleman acquaintance about improving the condition of under-privileged families, she will have had a similar snack at some good restaurant and will have danced enough to be fatigued and sleepy. The husband will therefore stay in his beddy-by. He will emit a tactful snore at intervals, to show that he is dead to the world.

The lady will show similar good manners by undressing with a minimum of noise. She will not shine the light long in his eyes. After she is in bed, it is quite *au fait* for her to arouse him and request him to go down and see if the garage door is locked, or to investigate a strong smell of gas coming up from the kitchen. Some of our most modern wives, however, prefer to let lying dogs sleep.

5

How to Get Up

THE naval command is "Hit the deck!" Among some soldiers, the word is "Show a leg!" It is undesirable to use either command at home. Only our native songbirds – little feathered friends of mankind – leap from their nests with a merry song to the rising sun. The higher animals, such as men and women, are at their grumpiest, ugliest and nastiest for several hours after sunrise.

You may, indeed, regard your wife as one of your "little friends in feathers and fur." Nevertheless, it is dangerous to romp with her, or try laughingly to drag her out of bed, when the alarm clock sounds its merry reveille in your home. If you roar "Show a leg!" in her ear, it will be called extreme mental cruelty at Reno.

In France, where such things are always done delicately, mothers bring their sleeping sons large cups of morning chocolate, to give them heart for the day. The stimulant most in use in this country is brandy and soda. Perhaps your mother obstinately refused to bring you this when you were a boy. Try to train your wife to do it. Such a refreshing morning draught will make you sing like a bird in your bath. Should you have any conscientious scruples against liquor in the early morning, the next best bet is tea or coffee. The wife who gets up half an hour before her husband and makes him a nice cup of tea to drink in bed will be gratefully remembered in his will. It is one case where etiquette pays dividends.

There are, alas, many wives who actually insist that their husbands shall get up first, close the window, and get out of the bathroom before they show a leg at all. If this occurs in your home, employ a servant and ring for him (or her) as soon as the alarm clock goes off. Say: "Tea and toast at once, damn you!" and go to sleep again.

We should warn you that, among social leaders and all other people of good breeding, the presence of servants in the bedroom is absolutely all right. You just don't notice them, except to swear at them. If you are bathing, and want a newspaper, shout for it until the houseman or the chambermaid hears you and brings it. Before you get up, have one or both of them pick up your clothes from the floor, draw your bath, lay out your clean underwear for the day, and bring your breakfast, as already described.

Only the absurd couples from the backwoods feel embarrassed by the presence of a servant when they are in bed, or doing their exercises, or hunting for lingerie under the bedclothes on the floor. Servants all became so tremendously hard-boiled, long ago, that they don't notice anything. You are no treat to them, whatever you do.

Like a lark springing out of its nest.

There are some little elegances in dressing, which a connoisseur of gracious living ought to know about. When putting on your pants (the fashionable word for trousers) be sure the servant holds the lower ends of them, so they won't pick up dust from the floor. If a woman, you must have the servant put on your stockings – put them on you, we mean. Sit in an easy attitude, with your foot thrust out. The servant will kneel in front of you, and you will feel like a queen. Don't kick, however, until your boots are on.

In old days, a gentleman was always shaved by his valet (pronounced valet). In these simpler times, he merely sends the valet running to the nearest drugstore for new blades. If you are visiting, your host and hostess will tell you, before you go bye-bye, to let them know if there's anything you want. Disregard this at the time. In the morning, however, it is a mark of breeding to send word by their servant that you want (1) a bottle of soda-water, (2) a new razor-blade, (3) a front collar stud, (4) a pair of golf shoes, and (5) a pair of thick stockings. Any other little items you require can be ordered at the same time.

One excellent rule, when visiting, is never to get up before lunch. This spares you the awful boredom that hangs over every country house in the morning.

PHYSICAL JERKS

Physical jerks is the amusing name for what some people call "setting-up exercises," or "callisthenics." They benefit a great many who were once pale and jaded. These people now run gymnasiums and sanatoriums, or are physical drill instructors at schools. If you are one of them, we agree that physical jerks are a swell thing for you, and will make you prosperous and rosy. Otherwise, they are a form of insanity which often attacks the strongest minds.

The first attack generally comes on the morning when, looking down your façade, you fail to see your knees. They have been eclipsed by a spherical body called the tum.

Such eclipses are common among men. But a man seldom waits for the period of total eclipse before endeavouring to improve his architecture. Paul du Chaillu, who discovered the gorillas in Africa, startled his audiences many years ago by saying that the male gorilla, or "Old Man," springs from his bed of leaves every morning and beats his inflated chest with his hairy fists until it booms like a drum.

Possibly your old man feels a similar impulse. If so, it is pitiable to have to lie in bed and watch him.

Yet you will not sleep. In his effort to do his daily dozen, he will knock over the lamp, sweep your favourite bric-a-brac off the mantelpiece and possibly knock the baby's tooth out.

It is not unlikely that your old man resembles a pear into which four matchsticks have been stuck. Nevertheless, he is quite sure that he will soon make himself look like a Greek athlete. Here is the daily dozen as practised, with this laudable purpose in view, by husbands in a majority of homes:

I – To get more exercise from the first movement, which is shaving, use a dull blade. Shave neatly, however. It is inconceivable to think of Apollo with a stubble on his jowls.

II – Take off the top of the pyjamas. This will automatically make a man feel like a victorious boxer, perhaps early Greek, or perhaps Benny Leonard or Jack Dempsey. Clench the fists, and look fierce. This is easy. You already look fierce.

III – Glance proudly at your manly form in the mirror. This will remind you to remove the stalactites of dried soap hanging from your ears.

Your knees have been eclipsed.

IV – If it is midwinter, throw open all the windows. The comfort of others must not stand in the way of clean, vigorous living.

V – Take a few deep breaths. Exhale through the mouth with a deep, hoarse, athletic sound.

VI – Lie flat on your back and see if you can set up again. (This explains the term, setting-up exercises.) Don't push with your hands till you have to.

VII – Place your hands on your hips. The command is "Hands on hips, place." Snap out this command to yourself in a military manner. Now bend your knees until you are sitting on your heels. Rise slowly and steadily. Repeat twenty-four times.

VIII – Lean against the wall, inhaling and exhaling rapidly, and noting your improved heart action. If you can't feel your heart throbbing, it isn't really working at full power for you.

IX – Lie on your face on the floor. Push yourself up with your hands, back arched. Go down again slowly. Repeat twenty-four times.

X, XI AND XII – Nobody has been able to remember or execute the three remaining exercises. Besides, you are now plenty late for breakfast.

When the husband has staggered back to the warm bathroom, leaving the bedroom windows healthily open, the wife may arise and take her own daily dozen. This can be done to music (hummed by the exerciser) and takes the form of stretching the arms and flinging them violently from right to left. If a tall daughter or son enters the room at this moment, let them learn to duck. Try winding your watch in front of the window, instead. This is light, agreeable exercise. On balmy days, the window may be slightly opened, but not to the extent of diverting the neighbours with a free athletic show.

HOW TO GET HIM TO STOP EXERCISING

If you have rashly married a former college athlete who will exercise every morning for years in the bedroom, and is not yet completely pear-shaped, your position is difficult. Does he choose a place where you can't move across the room without tripping over his body? Does he accompany himself with horrid groans? They all do.

Since tripping over the ruffian only amuses him, you must try subtler methods. While he is doing his push-ups, tell him softly that the plumber's bill is now twenty pounds. Remind him that the dentist's charge for straightening little Tommy's teeth is thirty pounds. This will divert his attention. If it doesn't, grab your clothes and dress in baby's room.

HOW TO MAKE CONVERSATION IN THE MORNING

One of the soundest rules for a couple who would have fun together is not to speak to one another until after breakfast.

There are, of course, cynics who recommend perpetual silence in matrimony. We believe this is going too far. There are undoubtedly moments when it is perfectly safe for each party to make conservative and carefully chosen remarks. It is before breakfast, however, that the seeds of many of the most baffling murder mysteries have been planted by a few seemingly innocent words. If you must talk during this dangerous hour devise some simple formulas. Never depart from them. Never reply to any question. We suggest short phrases like "It can't be as late as that!" "Missed my train again!" "Where the hell do my collars go to?" "Another lousy day!" "God, I'm tired!" "I wish it was night!" "If you knew how I felt!" etc.

Far better, however, to lie in silence during those last few minutes while you wait for your room-mate to shut the window. Wallow quietly in your own misery. Either that, or you will wallow in a greater one. Don't start the day with a conversation like this, addressed to the flies on the ceiling:

"Gosh, I'm tired."

"Yeah? Well, how do you think I feel?"

"Glad nobody's coming to dinner to-night."

"The Sealinghams are coming."

"What in hell did you want to ask them for?"

"I didn't. You asked them – a week ago."

"Of all the boring people I know, those two are the worst. I can't stand it. I'll tell them I'm sick, and go to bed."

"You'll do nothing of the kind. I think you're very mean. I don't say those things about your friends and I certainly could if I wanted to."

"We can't afford to go on feeding the community like this. My home is getting like a soup kitchen."

"It isn't the food bills. It's the stuff you pour into your friends."

"I've got to give them something. I drink their stuff, don't I? They wouldn't come if I didn't."

"I thought you didn't want them to come."

"I don't, but we've got to see somebody once in a while, or we'll go nuts."

"Well, I don't care what you do but I'm sick of being hounded about bills all the time. You always seem to have enough money to go to club dinners. God knows I spend my life scrimping and saving for you."

"We haven't begun to scrimp. I tell you if things keep on as they are going we'll all be in the workhouse. You women just don't understand how bad things are. If you had to go out and work, you'd – "

"I suppose you're going to tell me now I don't work."

"What do you do?"

"What do I do? I suppose hacking four children to school and back every day in an old car, and standing all the morning on one foot, shopping and paying bills, and trying to keep this house looking decent without enough help, is not work!"

"It doesn't sound like work to me. If I were a bachelor, now, I could run this whole show, kids and all, on one house boy and I'd have it running right too. I'd – "

But why go on. The day is ruined. No matter what you say next, it is wrong. The chances are that by ten o'clock you'll feel so badly that you'll spend a shilling calling her up from town to explain what a cad you are. You might as well save the money for a bootblack.

Silence is golden, saith the prophet. Yea, even at the present international price of gold.

6

Bathroom Rules

WE were taught at school that gin (Ark-wright's cotton gin) was the most important invention of the past three hundred years. This may be true. It is about the only kind of gin we have not tried recently. We believe, however, that the discovery of the bathroom has played an even more important part in our cultural life. Bathrooms were invented by the early Romans. Tubs came later, not being considered necessary until about 1860. Showers came later still.

The assembly of all these things into one convenient room, as public and refined as a dining-room or a living-room, did not take place until 1890-95. At that time it was good form to have only one bathroom in a house, and to place it as far as possible from the bedrooms. Usually it was in the ell, or back building. In these one-bathroom homes, entire families splashed about for years in complete harmony. Guests waited patiently for their chance to go to the bathroom. They peeped through cracks in bedroom doors until they felt more or less sure that Grandmother, Uncle George, Aunt Nettie, and the two daughters of the house had all finished their baths. Then the guests, in flannel wrappers and carrying sponges, razors, shaving soap, etc., went tiptoeing down the hall, hoping to find the door unlocked.

If not unlocked, they waited in the hall, discussing books or the weather. Just as the "end-seat hog" in a tram car was unpopular, so was the "bathroom hog." People washed quickly, cleaned out the tub and washbowl, and left the room in apple-pie order for the next comer. The mutual good will of men and women was never higher than in those one-bathroom days.

BIGGER AND BRIGHTER BATHROOMS

And then came the sanitary engineer. He took a long look at all the smart, up-to-date bathrooms of 1900. What did he see? He saw tin tubs, cased in imitation mahogany. He saw water closets that had known no aesthetic uplift since Queen Elizabeth's time. He saw ordinary clear glass windows, protected only by shades on cranky rollers. He saw no pretty wall cabinets, no purple shower curtains, no alluring plate glass mirrors on the walls and on the ceiling over the tub.

We regard all these things as absolute necessities in our homes to-day. Thank the engineer for them. He travelled abroad. He visited the Alhambra and the Taj Mahal.

These great works fired his imagination. He swore that every family should have a bit of the Alhambra and the Taj in their own home. The rest of our house or apartment may sag and crack. The paper may hang in great blisters and tatters from our bedroom walls. The cellar may be a swamp. But if our bathrooms look like a combination of a Sultan's seraglio and a modern drug store, the rest does not seem to matter.

When bathrooms lost their old utilitarian character and invaded the field of art, they also multiplied. Unhappy is the person to-day who cannot slip from any bedroom into the glare of a private bath. The old tin tub lies a-mouldering in the dump.

Gorgeous baths caused the fall of the Roman Empire. In his readable little book on that subject, the historian Gibbon says that the peak of luxury was reached in the Roman bath houses. Both sexes wallowed around together for hours every day. They dissolved their moral fibre in hot water. There is danger that history may be repeating itself. When a nation washes too easily it becomes decadent.

Our ancestors were so sturdy that they did not weaken themselves with hot water and soap and bath salts. An occasional swim on a warm summer's day was all the washing they cared about. The parts that didn't show didn't matter – and think how much time and money they saved. Spending as much time in private bathrooms as we do to-day, it is no wonder we can't keep them neat and orderly. The squdged toothpaste smears the glass shelf. Creamy mounds of shaving soap lie on the gleaming basin. Hairpins bristle in the soapdish. Corn plasters, fragments of lipstick, cigarette ends and pipe ashes lie upon the floor. Let us take warning before it is too late. At the dawn of this new era, let us review our bathroom manners before to-morrow's sun comes up. Its rays should not discover what a mess we have made of our little Taj Mahals.

In order to point the way, we offer a few simple rules.

Bathroom Rules

BATHROOM RULES AND BY-LAWS

1. Are you the proud owner of an enclosed shower? Then do not sing in it each morning until the last drop of hot water has gone rollicking down the drain. The Paul Robeson quality which you detect in your voice is apparent only to those inside the shower. To those on the outside it causes a definite lowering of the vitality, particularly before breakfast.

2. To many people a hot bath is like a cocktail. Upon emerging from a half-hour of thoughtful soaking they go into a temporary frenzy. In such moments they delight in throwing handfuls of talcum powder into the air. Fate is allowed to determine whether it shall fall on their bodies or upon the floor, the fixtures and your hair brushes. Restrain yourself.

3. If you must soak your gloves overnight in the hand basin, do something about unsoaking them in the early morning. Don't leave them, like a nest of pickled eels, to greet your man in the cold grey dawn.

4. The whole question of operating an amateur laundry in the bathroom should be given careful study. The chances are that Abelard, while scraping his beard, was not forced to regard languid rows of Heloise's damp stockings hanging from the towel horse and the bathroom rails.

5. When you take something from the medicine cupboard, put it back. Don't transfer its contents, item by item, to the bathroom shelf until the latter crashes into the basin.

6. If, for some strange reason, you feel jovial in the morning, keep it to yourself. Others are not in the same mood. You wouldn't think of singing at the top of your lungs in your early train or the underground. At least, you would only think of it once.

7. Do not try to carry on a conversation with someone while taking a shower. No matter what the original subject, you will always end by cursing one another.

8. Having completed your toilet, do not rush from a nice steamy bathroom into an ice cold bedroom leaving the door open behind you.

9. Never forget what a wonderful thing a wash-basin is. If you had to go down to the brook for a pail of water whenever you wanted to wash, you would realize this. (Either that, or you wouldn't wash.) Just because it is so convenient, however, it is abused. We therefore suggest a wash-basin code. It should be pasted on every bathroom mirror and read as follows:

- Don't leave a soapy rim in the bowl.
- Don't scatter flakes of dried sea-weed over its top.
- Don't clip your moustache over it.
- Don't leave safety pins and bits of ribbon lying on it.
- Don't leave the nail brush in it.
- Don't leave anything in it.

In conclusion, we may remind you that the whole purpose of recent legislation in America was to relieve the people of the burden of making gin in the tub. Now they can use it for goldfish.

7

Away from Home

BERTH CONTROL IN THE RAILWAY SLEEPING CAR

NOBODY knows when sleeping cars were invented. Art went modern twenty-five years ago. Furniture, motor-cars and morals have been modern for a long time. It is hardly conceivable, however, that anybody will ever have the nerve to modernize the sleeping car. When you enter an ordinary sleeping car, you have the same reverent feeling as at Stonehenge or the Pyramids. You know you are looking at the product of prehistoric times. Even if the car is built of steel, its design has not changed in the past fifty years. The steel itself is nicely grained to look just like wood.

You will notice, first, that the company encourages fun and intimacy among the guests. The builders have been clever enough to use green curtains, instead of the stupid solid walls that are customary in houses, hotels, and steamships. These curtains are not fastened with zippers. Just a few buttons are used. This is to entertain you and the other guests. Thanks to the curtains, you will have a jolly time peeping at one another, striking up friendships, and enjoying many a comical glimpse of the things that happen after people retire for the night.

Of course, they don't really retire. They are all in the same room, snoring, giggling, cursing, chatting, etc., behind their curtains. When a baby cries, everybody hears the little sufferer, and is sorry – at least for himself. If somebody is car-sick, the same wave of human sympathy travels through the car. You can readily hear all your neighbours changing their clothes. In fact you can almost hear them changing their minds.

A summer hotel built in this amusing and intimate way would be a side-splitting novelty. An ocean liner so constructed would be sunk by the weight of people rushing to board it. For some reason unknown to the authors, sleeping cars have never enjoyed the popularity they really deserve. This is possibly due to the fact that you pay the company a sum of money to ride in them, and not vice versa.

ENTRY INTO THE CAR

Lots of passengers, including old ladies, and tired business men who never walk a step otherwise, when boarding a train at a main railway station have to trudge merrily about a quarter of a mile before reaching their car. Walking is the best of exercise, of course. Inflate your chest, arch your spine, and enjoy it. Instruct the superintendent to stow your bag under your berth, give him a small piece of money, and wish him a pleasant walk back.

REFINEMENT IN THE CAR

Do not stop to admire your surroundings. Call the car porter at once. Have him excavate your bag from under the berth. Take out of it what comforts you have provided for the night, such as toothbrush, Mothersill's, bed socks, back numbers of newspapers, household ammonia, etc. Then recall the porter, and have him put the bag back.

Keep jingling the keys in your pocket. Make the porter perform all sorts of small, needless services. This will establish you in his eyes as a person of importance, from whom an immense tip can be confidently expected.

Pretend that you yourself are an important public

man or, if a lady, that great man's wife. The first rule of good breeding in a sleeping car is never to do any work yourself. Look majestic. It is probably the only chance you will ever have to do this, so take full advantage. If you require the conductor, that worthy will be in the station lunch counter, flirting with the barmaid over a bun, but you are not supposed to know this.

ETIQUETTE FOR ALL PASSENGERS

Maybe you are an old-fashioned person who likes to go to the washroom before going to bed, instead of just rolling in without tiresome preparations, as truly modern people do. In this case, take your toothbrush, etc., and go to the end of the car marked "Gentlemen" or "Ladies," as the case may be. If a lady, you will find the washroom to be one-quarter of the size of the gentlemen's room. Whether males wash four times as much, or occupy four times the amount of space, is one of science's unsolved problems.

Small as the ladies' room is, it will look smaller because already occupied by a middle-aged blonde, an old lady and two fatigued lady buyers from department stores, who are having a little nip and a cigarette before retiring. The middle-aged blonde will be a chorus girl, and the old lady a minister's wife making her first overnight trip. The five of you will have an intimate time picking each other's cigarettes, powder rags and combings out of the wash-basin. The first woman who busts into the larger, more airy, and cleaner men's washroom will be a hero of her sex, just as much as Joan of Arc was. There are no decencies in a sleeping car, anyway. But the attendant keeps the men's end fairly clean.

Washed, delicately anointed and perfumed for the night, you may now slip into a becoming negligée and walk gracefully to your berth. If you trip over the stockinged feet of the fat man in Lower 11, tell him to pull in his neck. The attendant will eventually end your discussion by bringing you the ladder, up which you will mount to a good night's sleep, and pleasant dreams. Ascend the ladder gracefully. Don't pay attention to the stolid gaze of the three professional football players, who are sitting in Lower 12 with the curtain open. Their remarks are never worth hearing. Pitch into your berth head first, roll over, and shut your curtains if you can get the hooks unsnarled on the pole. If any buttons are left, it is a mark of refinement to button them.

Take your undressing in easy stages. Try to avoid getting panicky. A wounded adder can always shed its

Plenty of comforts for the night.

skin, and you can readily undress in an upper berth if
you remember how it is done. It is just a knack. You
will learn it all the faster if the night happens to be
bitterly cold. Then, just as you get down to the last
piece, you remember that your pyjamas are not

with you. They are packed neatly in your bag far, far below. Ring for the attendant. Stick your head out through the curtains. You will see nothing but the sinister swinging of other curtains, with strange elephant-like bumps moving behind them, where your brother and sister passengers are going to bed.

Keep calm, although your teeth are chattering. Ring again. Ring many times. Hysteria now begins to get you. Suppose there should be a railway accident just at this minute. A fine condition you are in, for a wreck! About this time the train usually slows down for a station. The attendant appears, and tells you that as soon as the train starts again, he will be with you. Half a dozen people now get on. All appear to be more or less cocked up. A stout gentleman, fresh and merry from a banquet of his Lodge, has a bluish ticket calling for your berth. He is the type of experienced traveller who gets what he has paid for. He tosses his despatch-case on to your shivering torso. You toss it back on his head.

The conductor is called in to umpire. After long discussion, your opponent is led away.

The attendant, now all attention, hands up your bag. You locate your missing pyjamas, put them on, and crawl gratefully between the sheets. The bag stays with you, this time.

FINAL NICETIES OF TRAVEL

During the night strange things will happen. Nobody knows why trains act as they do at night. By day they bumble along as sedately as steam-rollers. Once the passengers are stowed away at night, trains lose all control of themselves. In hilly country, through numerous cuttings, they dash along like chain lightning, lurching from side to side, with the whistle screaming. On the level, however, they lose all ambition, and try to stop at every milestone. At some stations a veteran employee bangs on the wheels of your car with a sledge hammer.

This gives you a fine sense of security. So does the excited man who runs up and down the platform shouting: "Okay! All right!" Between stops the train acts like a nervous gun dog, now nosing forward, now stopping suddenly dead. Old travellers keep their heads from marring the partition, when this happens, by wearing crash helmets. For a lady, a hard felt hunting hat with reinforced crown is always chic.

Then at last comes the dawn. Dawn on a sleeping car doesn't come up like thunder. It has no rosy fingers. The porter simply turns on the aisle light in your eyes. You will probably now go soundly to sleep for the first time, and awake only after a series of intimate pinches from the porter.

The washroom will be just as it was the night before, with the addition of more cigarette ends, powder rags, or (if in the gentlemen's end) used shaving lather. Wash your hands until they turn from the dark shade called "elephant grey" to the fashionable shade called "beige." Never mind your neck and ears. They will have to be boiled when you get home – or sand-blasted. By the time your toilet is finished the train will have been in the station five minutes. You will have the pleasure of repacking your bag while the boys who play football force themselves past your obstinate hind-quarters. Don't hurry. Wait until you think the porter has gone home to see his family. Then dash for the platform. He will meet you, however, at the vestibule and wrench your bags from you, exclaiming "Brush you off?" Say to him: "No, I will get off in the regular manner." This is an old retort, but true and tried. While he is figuring out a reply, make a tremendous jangling of coins and keys. When his palm comes forward, pour a fistful of your smallest change into it. Grab your bag and run. If you are spry you will be out of sight before he counts up and finds the total sum.

CAMP-BED MANNERS

We don't propose to do more than touch on this subject. Every phase of camp life has been all too fully covered, both seriously and flippantly. It is high time to bury the subject. During the Genteel Era before the War, camping was the only way by which respectable writers might approach the subject of sleep. In those days ladies and gentlemen did not go to bed at night – they retired. How they did it was nobody's business. An author who thought differently would have found himself excluded from the circulating library.

It was only during those brief periods when cultured people elected to spend a brief night in the deep, deep woods that literature was permitted to see them as human beings who actually slept and – pardon the indiscretion – appeared dishevelled at dawn.

It is with a feeling of donning pantalettes, therefore, that we approach the subject. Yet we are too timid to omit it. Having been ourselves born in the Genteel Era, a book on bedroom manners which did not touch on the etiquette of the camp fire would be inconceivable.

As a matter of fact, camps are apt to be the one place where our manners are at their best – granting, of course, that there is more than one couple in the camping party. It is an axiom of human conduct that when two or three couples are gathered together each male spends his time trying to impress all the other females (wife excepted) and vice versa. The result is that everyone acts quite unnaturally, and the total effect is polite and charming. There are a few pointers, however, which are well worth keeping in mind.

Squealing will lose you all your friends.

I – Remember that, although a man's efforts to attract the opposite sex are both natural and inevitable, there is no profit in driving your own wife, and the men of the party, to the point of homicide.

II – If you are a female, remember that squealing about vermin, whether actual or imaginary, will cause you to lose all of your women friends immediately. If continued far enough into the night it will eventually estrange all living creatures, except the vermin.

III – Remember that there are some people capable of sleeping even under the most sordid conditions. If you are so constituted that the woods intoxicate you and make you giggle, don't wait until everyone is nested down before you begin. Should you be a confirmed camp-bed giggler, try getting into your roll head first.

IV – Don't eat jam or onions before blowing up air mattresses.

V – Don't spring up at the first trace of dawn to chop kindling wood and rattle pails. Bear in mind that you are not on a scientific exploring expedition. A little slackness at this time of morning will win you many warm friends.

VI – Do you feel wakeful after the last drink of coffee? If so, don't wait until everyone is dozing off before sticking your head out of the blankets to ask "Is everybody asleep?" Should you be the kind of a person who must ask this question, do so early when the answer is decidedly "No," or later when they can't hear you.

VII – If you are a woman – be yourself. Avoid spending the first hour of the morning painting your face while the others cook and eat breakfast. On the other hand, don't get the idea that because you are in the woods you must look like an unwashed female clown. If you do this you are sure to find yourself with the odd girl at the portages.

VIII – If you have picked yourself a nest of roots for your bed, don't twitch and groan all night. Focus on two things. First, everyone else is equally uncomfortable. Second, this is only going to last one night. After that, vow never to make such an ass of yourself again.

Then remember your vow and put an end to these camping party things for ever.

BED MANNERS IN A COUNTRY HOUSE

You are speeding through woods that look as if they'd been gone over with a vacuum cleaner. Every leaf clean and glossy, not a speck of underbrush. You see a herd of deer. Then a cock pheasant rises from the road, with a whirr of its expensive wings.

"How long before we get to the – er – estate?" you ask.

"We've been on the estate for the past 'alf-'our, sir," answers the flunkey. "You may now catch a glimpse of the main 'ouse."

You do. It stuns you. Windsor Castle, but on a larger scale. Peacocks are strutting on its parterres. Now you have whizzed through the village, and past an artifical lake – a large one. Windsor Castle is out of sight now, but you are drawing up in front of a large building in the French style. You are shown to the Marie Antoinette suite, a nest of silk hangings and gilt furniture. Since you are too late for lunch at the main 'ouse, a pleasant little four-course dejeuner is to be served in your own dining-room. Footmen are standing behind the chairs where you and Susie will sit. Alas, for your sensible, simple holiday!

Away from Home

Your alarming valet has by now unpacked you. He has laid out your smelly shooting clothes, your torn sweater, and your woollen socks with large holes in their toes. And what has he laid them out on? True to his traditions, he has laid them on a Bed – a Bed with a capital B. It stands on a raised platform. It is a monstrous concoction of gold scrollwork, painted panels, and heavy silk canopies. Instead of bedposts, it has figures of cupids embracing nymphs. It is so high that an ornate little gilt stepladder is provided to mount it.

At this moment you must make a great decision. Either you and Susie can bluff things out, and try to find among the eighty-nine other guests dotted over many square miles of estate a couple of good Samaritans who will lend you the necessary wardrobes – or else, you can beat it at once. Let's assume you have no friends whatever among the guests, that you are too proud to try to borrow a suit from Ponsonby, the valet (who is twice your size, anyway), and that you want to make a decent get away.

IF YOU ARE POOR BUT PROUD

Summon Ponsonby. He will come to you with a silly remark about being unable to find your evening clothes. "White ties are being worn to-night," he will say.

Pay no attention. Think of a town and think of a telephone number – no matter which and what. If you can't think, Westminster is an impressive place, and Whitehall 1212 is a serviceable number. Instruct Ponsonby to call that number, and to inform the First Secretary that Mr. Thomas Turtlebottom will be with him to-morrow. That will take Ponsonby down a couple of pegs. Have him call up the garage for the station waggon, have him repack your rags, give him as little as your conscience permits, and ho! for the junction and any old train you can catch. Susan will regret in after life that she never did sleep in that bed. But she can't have everything!

IF YOU ARE POOR BUT SHAMELESS

In any big house party you can always find somebody you know. It will probably prove to be those awful De Bracy Finkenvillers, whom you haven't spoken to at Scarsdale for ten years. You will now find them lolling in luxury. Go right up and fall on De Bracy's neck.

"Enfin" French for "at last."

If you manage things well, you will emerge from this happy reunion with De Bracy's dinner jacket, with his second-best Burberry, half a dozen of his shirts, his spare pair of braces, and an absolutely foul assortment of his ill-chosen jewellery and ties. Thank Providence for this rich haul. If Susie has equal luck with Mrs. Finkenvillers, you needn't 'phone that appointment till to-morrow. You will have a night in Marie Antoinette's bed.

Do justice to the occasion. Conduct yourself with fitting gallantry. Brush up your French. When at three o'clock in the morning you come back, exhausted, from dinner and bridge and music and dancing in the main 'ouse, tell Susan what she wants to hear. Tell her that her eyes outshone all the candles in the great hall, or that Mrs. Finkenvillers' horrid old dress didn't show any gap in the back.

Your French may not suffice for these elaborate compliments, but don't let that stop you. You know your Susan. Make a little ceremony of helping her up the gilt ladder. When you give your hand to steady her, say "Enfin!" (French for "at last!"). When she wants to climb down in the morning, say "Dejà?" (French for "so soon?"). Susan will give a little squall of surprise at finding the bed is made up with black silk sheets. That is because Louis XVI was so tired of seeing women in white ones. Tell her this interesting historical fact. Be as much like an old-time courtier as you can. You may look anything but romantic when you take off De Bracy's black clothes and stand revealed in your old slumber suit – far too tight around the waist and too baggy in the seat. But wear it with a flourish, as D'Artagnan would have done.

These chivalrous new manners of yours will remain a pleasant memory, when you recall your first (and last) visit to Heart's Ease. With slight logical revisions, they will also make a tremendous hit at home.

IF YOU AREN'T POOR AT ALL

Maybe you are as rich as your host Mr Hart, every whit. Maybe you sized him up for a pleasant little plebeian, with no more millions than he has fingers and toes. This is most unlikely. A multi-millionaire can recognize another on sight, if not sooner. Their shabby clothes and shyness deceive all bourgeois people, but don't fool each other. Put two of them in any crowd, and they will soon be hobnobbing together. If one of them speaks to you, he will ask some unimportant question like "How is your mother, nowadays?" But if he has anything important to ask, he will prowl around till he finds another millionaire and then he will say: "Do you know what time it is?" or "Have you got a match?" It seems as if he could accept important information, or any small favour, only from one of his own kind. Don't ask us why. Birds of a feather flock together. This applies only to multis – not to the common millionaires you meet everywhere, who dress as flamboyantly and talk as noisily as if they hadn't a bean.

Well, if you are a multi, and if you went down to see Hart, you wouldn't bother a minute with the Marie Antoinette bed. It would make you dizzy to lie in it. You would tell the house man you can sleep only on an army cot. Or any old bedstead without box springs will do. Would you bother about clothes? Not at all. Of course, you could telephone to your town house to have a full wardrobe motored out to Gatwick Airport, and from there your private pilot could fly it down to you in time for dinner. But you'd just moon around the grounds all afternoon, being largely mistaken for a plumber or for the man who gives the baby pheasants their Mellen's Food.

Hart would find you at last – behind a toolshed – and the two of you would hold a nice long intimate conversation, leading up to the point that you will dine together in your shooting clothes, and that your favourite dinner is hamburger steak, pretzels, and beer.

Then you can go to bed comfortably on the cot, and slide out early next morning for your own little place in the country.

8

How to be a Charming Invalid

THE CHARMING INVALID AT HOME

This can't be done. But you may have to attempt it, none the less. You have made up your mind bravely to endure your next illness in your little white bed at home. Your ancestors were born, slept, lived much of their lives and finally died economically in their own beds. Why can't you? You can! In fact, you must. So here is a brief and, we hope, not too terrifying outline of your next disease.

THE ILLNESS

Dr. Rooby advises you to stay in bed, to avoid using your eyes too much, and to live largely on liquid food.

Well, if this is the end, you can at least die game.

You suggest to him that whisky is a food. He shakes his head.

Your wife's expression has changed. She clearly realizes that for the next week she will have to wait hand and foot on a fully grown man with a nursery disease. Just as this glad thought comes to her, Bridget taps on the door and admits a bespectacled hag with a suitcase. "The trained nurse," announces Bridget.

Dr. Rooby takes the nurse away in his car. This is a break. With so much real disease around – like the 'flu – young and pretty nurses have been all snapped up. Besides, there's nothing the matter with you. You absorb a large bowl of soup, a dozen biscuits, and a couple of doughnuts. Hurrah for the chance to lie lazily in bed, reading a thrilling new novel in print so large it doesn't hurt your poor, bloodshot eyes. By the end of the second day, you are wondering why there is no decent reading matter in the house. You can't decide whether to re-read Ivanhoe or Goodwin's Greek Grammar. That's the worst of trying to read in bed all day, it makes your head ache. If you were only at a hospital, you would have some visitors. But nobody calls on a man who has measles at home.

You discover, meanwhile, that your home is a veritable throbbing hive of human activity, all day long. In the morning you hear the endless Whoo-hoo-hoo-oo of the electric vacuum cleaner. Why can't Bridget use a brush, and some elbow grease, and help cut down your electric bills? Thank the Lord the doorbell operates on a battery. It rings all the time. There are hundreds of callers and Bridget holds long converse with each one. You have, by this time, stopped answering the telephone, although it offers you many extraordinary opportunities to buy furniture, hardware, groceries, insurance, stocks and shares, annuities and other things. And you find the wireless bringing you its messages more furiously, even, than it does in the evening. Your wife remains calm, goes to her favourite place for morning coffee and her various afternoon clubs and bridge classes.

SOME "DON'TS" FOR THE HOME INVALID

During all this long visit to your own home, you will naturally find many things to criticize. Don't. Here are some remarks which a well-behaved invalid will never make to his wife while she is trained-nursing him at home:

1. This soup tastes so good it must have come out of a tin.

2. My mother used to have the laundry done at home, and my pyjamas were never torn to tatters.

3. These sheets must have come from a manufacturer of emery cloth, didn't they?

4. I don't understand why you let the children use such awful language. When they were playing in the garden this afternoon, I heard them say

things which would have shocked the man who can shoe an army mule. Why don't you do something about it?

5. How about persuading Bridget to take a bath, now summer has come.

6. I don't see why you have to spend all this afternoon pouring out tea for Mrs. McAtooty-Paramore's guests. This is the first afternoon for six years I haven't been out slaving for my family.

Such remarks are dangerous. Suppose your wife stops pampering you and turns on you. Your wife can be goaded just so far. She may reply that if you have slaved intelligently, she could hire a great chef to make your soup and could buy your sheets from a silk manufacturer. What snappy comeback can you think of for that? But she will probably feel that sheer logic puts you out of your depth at once. Her best instinct is to keep you so well supplied with food, cigarettes, newspapers, cheap magazines, sensational novels, and all sorts of amusing small objects from a trick, joke and puzzle shop, that you won't have much time to talk. This is why she pampers you. A hospital will not.

HOW TO MAKE A HOSPITAL
PROUD OF YOU

We have described the sensations of any ordinarily sensitive man who sets out to be ill at home. His bed manners are really his own affair. In the early stages of his malady, the best he can do is to keep out of the poached egg and marmalade. In the later stages, people are waiting on him all the time – rushing upstairs with his beef-tea and biscuits, consulting his whims, and pandering to his tastes and appetites. No hospital can do this.

A hospital refers to you always as a "patient." And you'd better be patient. Think of yourself as a nut on the way through a large motor-car factory. Your whims are no more interesting to the hospital than the whims, etc., of the late Alaric the Goth. You are in the hospital to be questioned, weighed, washed, charted, carted, anaesthetized, operated on, medicated, weighed, washed, charged, dressed and discharged.

People in hospitals divide sharply into two classes. The first class loves everything that befalls to them – from the first questionnaire about your age, sex, name of person to notify, etc., straight through to the high, hard, narrow, hospital bed, and the exciting hospital smell that is a blend of rubber matting, stale orchids, carbolic acid, freshly starched uniforms and formaldehyde, with a soupcon of chicken soupcon. Such people sit up chirpily in their beds, beaming with self-importance on their visitors. When they leave the hospitals they write magazine articles on "My Operation." If the magazines by any chance don't accept the articles, they still secure far wider circulation by telling all the details to everybody they meet.

Weighed, washed, charted, carted.

The other kind of people dislike hospitals. The idea that some people want peace and rest in a bustling hospital, full of efficiency and rules, makes every member of the hospital staff see red. (Well, not every member. There are a few glorious exceptions, as we shall prove.) But most of them have got the idea that this is the assembly line at a motor-car works in boom days. If they aren't rolling you from side to side to wash you and make your bed, they are making you write your luncheon order, or combing your hair, or asking you intimate questions and writing the answers on a "chart' which they pin up somewhere in plain sight of every visitor who is at all curious to look – your own visitors, and other people's.

Try and get the sister to hang on your door-knob one of those hotel signs which read "Do Not Disturb." She won't know what you are talking about. You are there to be disturbed. And for your own good. So it all boils down to a final test – a veritable Doctor of Philosophy examination – of your bed manners.

If you can smile in a well-bred way when they come in, when night is blackest, to weigh you; if you can sit up and brilliantly entertain any visitor who has nowhere else to go; if you never ring your bell; if you don't expect the hospital to be interested in your case and your whims – why, you have all the bed manners anybody needs to become a prime favourite in the very biggest modern hospital.

Be unconscious as much as you can. Don't expect the whole staff and the board of trustees to be impressed because you have lost your appendix. You'll have to lose your whole table of contents to intrigue them. Answer your 'phone calls promptly. Buy, without much argument, whatever they offer you, from brushes to bonds. If you argue, it will disturb the old lady next door. It may even increase your temperature, and make your chart too interesting.

Don't discuss your case with your nurse. Discuss her case. There is sure to be a man in it, somewhere. Eat far more than you want at every meal — even people with the best medical training share the old superstition that this is good for you. Even if you think you are at your last gasp, don't be annoyed if you hear the ward nurse saying to an inquirer: "Yes, her condition seems very much improved to day." Don't throw the glass water-jug at the nurse if she says: "She had a very comfortable night." After all, what kinder things could the poor girl say to your kind friends?

Persevere along these lines. You will eventually find that someone in the hospital has a human heart. It may be your own nurse. It may be the engineer's assistant, who comes to bang on your radiator at five a.m. It may be a grey-haired man who comes in to clean the place. He may suddenly decide that it ain't right for anybody to be sufferin' like what you are. If so, he will go and sneak you something from the cupboard where the drinks are kept – and quite likely save your life.

THE PROBLEM OF FLOWERS

This is a minor problem to most people, till they get into hospital. A bowl of daffodils or a window box of petunias may supply all the botany you want when you are at home.

In the hospital, however, you will probably find yourself lying in a jungle of azaleas, roses, lilies, zinnias, orchids, and other blooms. You can have them sent to the public ward, if their mixed fragrance combines unpleasantly with the fumes of your recent anæsthetic. Few people have the courage of a popular débutante, who asked her friends to send cheques instead. She informed the friends that these cheques would be devoted to her favourite charity. They were.

If you can't bring yourself to realize that charity begins at home, you might have your secretary call up every florist in town, and ask him to give you credit for the flowers instead of the actual blooms. Then you can thriftily use the credit for your own Easter and Christmas gifts, or the like. However, you have to be a person who absolutely terrifies all florists to do this. The chances are that you'll just have to look like a small, sick monkey in a large conservatory, until the avalanche of floral offerings comes to a stop. It is seldom embarrassing in size after the first four days. By that time most of your friends will be feeling the well-established human desire that you will get well, or something.

9

Simple Rules for Subtle People

THE pages that follow describe and give common sense cures for all the usual causes of bedroom distress. Why not read one section every night before turning out the reading lamp. Read it aloud, if you dare.

KILLING MOSQUITOS

The only thing more annoying than a mosquito is a mosquito-killer. Some people have an ear for a mosquito like a Sioux Indian. Let one but stick his head into the room (the mosquito, of course) and such a person is out of bed as if propelled by a spring. The attack always commences when you are gliding off into your first blissful slumber. You are awakened by a sudden oath, sadly out of place on refined lips. The light snaps on. Your mate, eyes glittering with blood lust, stands on the bed, your most private garment screwed up in her hand. Such a person will battle all night. No quarter is asked or given. Once the combat starts, there are no bounds or rules.

Let the hunted creature take refuge on the ceiling over your head. You have only time to brace yourself before you are stepped on. Then you hear a thud against the ceiling. If you see a blood spot, this counts as six points, or a touchdown. The black and blue spot on your torso counts one point, whether the mosquito dies or not. If you must kill mosquitoes sleep in the guest room during the open season.

MONEY

Never talk about money until after breakfast. It is even more important not to mention the lack of it on an empty stomach.

THE ALARM CLOCK

If two people want to live harmoniously they should vie with one another in tending the alarm clock. Each day should end with a friendly tussle for the privilege of winding the blasted thing – and also setting it, for it is always fifteen minutes fast or slow.

Some clever man will eventually invent a Twin Bed Special alarm clock, with a face on the back as well as on the front. As it is now, one partner always wants to be able to note the passing of time all through the night. The other, in consequence awakes at six and lies miserably until seven wondering what time it is, and too cold to reach out and turn the clock round. The sneakiest trick of all is quietly to reverse it in your direction under cover of darkness.

TOWELLING

If you are smart and thrifty enough to use towels twice, fold them neatly.

Having settled this point, hold a conference and decide, once and for life, the manner of folding. This is particularly true of bath towels. Most men prefer to fold them like a horse blanket. Women like to fold them as they were in the box when they came.

It doesn't make much difference. Only get together on it. Women have a feminine liking for looking at their initials while lolling in the tub.

SLIPPERS

If you are going to wear bedroom slippers – wear them. Don't drag them around after you with your toes as if you were playing a comedy part in Uncle Tom's Cabin.

FACE FLANNELS

These, particularly the other fellow's, must not be used for the following purposes:

1. Cleaning the hand basin
2. Shining patent leather shoes with your wife's face cream
3. Scouring the soap dish
4. Killing spiders
5. Whitening tennis shoes.

LAST-MINUTE MEN

At the end of thirty-five years, most men should have a fair idea of how long it takes them to shave, bath and dress. Few ever acquire this, however. Each dawn brings the fresh hope of beating all past records. As a result, many a man who has not caught the 8.07 for ten years continues to speak of it as his regular train.

Cultivate the habit of allowing yourself at least thirty-five seconds leeway each morning for unexpected occurrences. As long as you lie in bed for twenty minutes after the alarm sounds, dressing and breakfast will be full of fun and colour. What a picture of manly dignity. Having lain like a listless flounder until the last minute, you suddenly spring out of bed with the expression of a maniac. Everything must now give way to the objective of getting Papa on his train. Your little ones recoil from your flying form in fear.

In the bathroom you tear and scrape at your face as if you would rip it from your skull. Into the bath and out you seethe, leaving a trail of soapy brushes, razor blades, and damp towels. Now you are hurling yourself into your clothes, buttoning with one hand, tying with another. You can't find your pocketbook. Half a dozen hands search frantically through the pockets of your other suit while you scream directions.

The maid knows your habits better. She counts on them. Your orange juice is on the table. As you gulp it down like castor oil she slides a dish of cereals before you. Your coffee has been standing on the sideboard for ten minutes. It is flanked by a special ration of leathery toast made a half-hour before. You hurl the loathsome objects into you, casting angry glances at your family the while.

Out comes the watch. Missed the 8.07 again. No one seems surprised. Their surprise will come the day you catch it. Implanting a peck on the dear one's forehead (her mouth being occupied with fresh toast), you bound from the house. As the door slams, your family heaves a sigh of relief. They can spend the rest of the day resting and fortifying their nerves against your return.

WINDOW BLINDS

There are some people who always cause the most obedient window blind to act like an army mule. Nothing is more distressing, at the end of an imperfect day, than to listen to a hand-to-hand struggle between one of these unfortunates and a blind. The end is always the same. Even though you have to pay for replacements, it is a relief when the thing is either torn from its pole, or crashes to the floor, to be left for the maid to throw away in the morning.

LAUNDRY

Modern parents have made big strides in educating their children in the Facts of Life. Much human misery would be eliminated, however, if every father would take his boy aside at a suitable age, and talk to him frankly on the subject of Laundry.

"My son," he should say, "some day you will yourself have a family. Nay, do not hang your head in shame. You will be merely following the way of all flesh. When that day comes, remember one thing, my boy. Never, during those happy years, will you be able to understand where your shirts and collars, underclothes and socks disappear to. Do not try. These are things that no man can comprehend. Above all, say nothing of your bereavement to the sweet girl whom you will eventually marry. It may seem to you an innocent thing to remark occasionally upon the depreciation in your laundry. That is because you do not yet understand women. There is nothing they resent more than the insinuation that your laundress is the ringleader of the Forty Thieves. Far better to be happy, and restock your wardrobe each month, than to make the slightest attempt to discover what becomes of it in the wash. The most you should do by the way of protest is to appear occasionally at breakfast without a collar. Remember, my son, that for reasons neither of us are old enough to understand, a man and his wash are soon parted."

WHO CLOSES THE WINDOW
ON COLD MORNINGS

This is one of those eternal questions without any immediate answer. Abstinence League statisticians, who used to spend their time calculating the working hours lost through Sunday drinking, might well turn their attention to this problem. We believe that the hours lost waiting for one's pillow-pal to get up and close the window would far exceed the hours lost playing about with the demon rum. It is doubtful if civilization has reached a point where any rulings can be made. It is just a catch-as-catch-can proposition – including colds in the head.

TINY LITTLE HABITS

Let drops of water fall on a block of granite long enough and the granite loses the fight. When you find yourself doing little eccentric things in the bedroom – watch yourself. If you find yourself doing them often – cast them from you. Otherwise they will eventually submerge you.

No discussion of tiny little habits would be complete without at least a mention of snoring. Of all the grossly insulting sounds indulged in by divinely created man, snoring is the gang leader. With unusual restraint we forbear from adding further to the mountain of literature on the subject already in existence. The only place where most recumbent men will ever learn to stop snoring is the tomb.

Sucking through the teeth, even as a sign of intense thought, should be punishable by fine or imprisonment or preferably both. Why it should be supposed to aid thought we do not know. We doubt, however, if Plato, Ruskin or Socrates ever found it helpful to make such noises whilst philosophizing.

We once knew a man, a charming fellow in every other respect, who for twenty years ran from his bath to his bedroom, holding his pyjamas before him like a speciality dancer and exclaiming "My God, how cold it is!" The habit became so deeply rooted that he did it on the hottest days of summer. He was eventually drowned by falling off one of the United Fruit Company's banana boats.

It is not advisable.

147

We know of another equally attractive person, also male, who, in the twilight zone of dawn, is apt to fill his lungs with air which he lets out bit by bit, accompanied by a gruesome grinding from what is known in the trade as the thoracic cavity. He disclaims all knowledge of the trick but that is not a valid excuse to his hearers.

Pressing the trousers under the mattress is useful and economical, but presents you each night in a most undignified attitude. There are so many other opportunities to look like a monkey that it is not advisable to put on a regular show.

Humming is bad. An occasionally happy little hum can do no harm. Habitual humming is to be deplored, however. Defiant humming is beyond excuse. The partner who cannot refrain from ending every argument with a little hum should go out in the yard and sleep in a dog kennel.

If you must clear your throat each morning, take it off by itself somewhere. If it is one of those throats which require constant clearing, you might try opening it up with a razor blade.

There is no place where you create a more regular routine than in the bedroom. Conditions there vary less than in any other phase of our daily life. Day after day – year after year – shaving succeeds teeth brushing, exercise follows shaving, bathing follows exercise. Later in the day the best planned time-tables are shot to pieces. We storm and fume, little realizing that the very irregularity which we deplore keeps us sane.

We know a man who was recently threatened with a nervous breakdown. Wisely he went to his family physician before consulting a specialist. Among the seemingly irrelevant facts that the doctor pulled out of him was that he followed an undeviating routine from the time he got up until the time he arrived at his office.

Instead of sending him to a mental home the doctor ordered a complete break-up of this morning routine. If he usually rose at seven he was now to rise at every hour but seven, from dawn till noon. Sometimes he was to shave after breakfast, sometimes the night before. Sometimes he was to grow a beard. He either arrived at his office in time to greet the scrub women, or to say good night to his departing partners. At first, this made him even more nervous. In a month he was cured. Avoid tiny little habits. Avoid routine. Neither has a place in good bed manners or in good living.

Last Words

WE HAVE called attention to a much neglected phase of manners. It is our belief that, just as charity begins at home, so should manners begin in the bedroom. It is our observation that most of them begin at the foot of the front stairs (going down) and end at the same place (going up). If we have succeeded in suggesting a few of the difficulties arising from this situation, the purpose of this book has been accomplished.

Unfortunately, national priggishness has prevented discussion of this problem in public forums. We have noticed, however, that whenever it is brought up in intimate circles, the light of interest gleams in every eye. All wish to talk at once. Each one desires to express a particular abhorrence. The shoe seems to fit every foot.

The sterling modesty of the authors has caused them to treat the subject with a degree of lightness. We are convinced, however, that bad bedroom manners affect not only the participants but *the entire world*. No government archives will ever disclose how some act of pre-breakfast nastiness on the part of a Prime Minister's wife has changed the history of a nation. No one will ever know how many wars have been prolonged because the commanding general preferred to remain on the field of battle (or a few miles behind it) rather than return to his conjugal bedchamber.

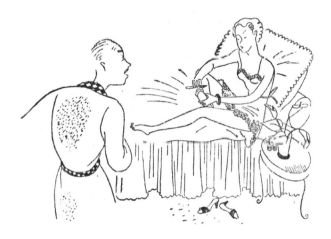

Has your loved one some little mannerism?

And so –

as the great diarist said –

To BED.